# TUNNEL RATS

# TUNNEL RATS

The larrikin Aussie legends who
discovered the Vietcong's secret weapon

Jimmy Thomson with Sandy MacGregor

Much of the material in this book, including interviews with the men of 3 Field Troop, was originally gathered by author Jimmy Thomson for Sandy MacGregor's self-published book *No Need For Heroes*. Sandy has since added material from his own archives and research, which has been included in this version of the story, now presented as a military history rather than a personal memoir.

First published in 2011


Allen & Unwin
Sydney, Melbourne, Auckland, London

83 Alexander Street
Crows Nest NSW 2065
Australia
Phone: (61 2) 8425 0100
Fax: (61 2) 9906 2218
Email: info@allenandunwin.com
Web: www.allenandunwin.com

Cataloguing-in-Publication details are available
from the National Library of Australia
www.trove.nla.gov.au

ISBN 978 1 74237 489 5

Map of Vietnam by Ian Faulkner
Set in 12/18 pt AIProsperall by Post Pre-press Group, Australia
Printed in Australia by McPherson's Printing Group

10 9 8 7 6 5 4 3 2 1

# CONTENTS

*To Corporal Bob Bowtell, who died in the tunnels at Ho Bo Woods, Cu Chi, South Vietnam, in January 1966. To all those soldiers who served with 3 Field Troop Royal Australian Engineers, September 1965 to September 1966, and all the Tunnel Rats, Australian and American, who followed them into the Vietcong's underground cities.*

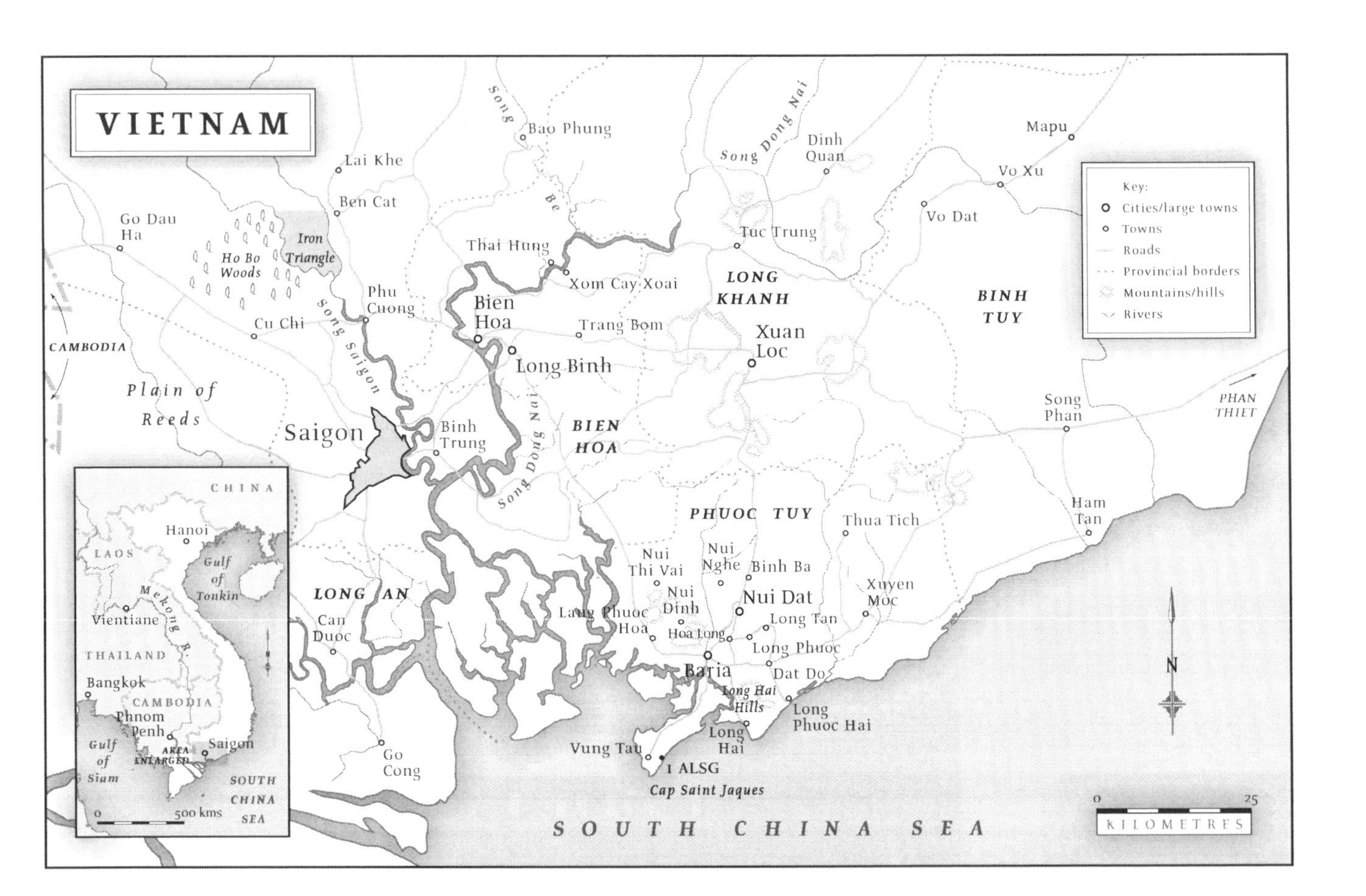
VIETNAM
Key:
Cities/large towns
Towns
Roads
Provincial borders
Mountains/hills
Rivers
Go Dau Ha
Ho Bo Woods
Iron Triangle
Lai Khe
Ben Cat
Bao Phung
Song Be
Song Dong Nai
Dinh Quan
Mapu
Vo Xu
Vo Dat
Tuc Trung
Thai Hung
Xom Cay Xoai
LONG KHANH
BINH TUY
Phu Cuong
Cu Chi
CAMBODIA
Bien Hoa
Trang Bom
Xuan Loc
Long Binh
Plain of Reeds
Song Saigon
Saigon
Binh Trung
BIEN HOA
Song Phan
PHAN THIET
Ham Tan
PHUOC TUY
Thua Tich
Nui Thi Vai
Nui Nghe
Binh Ba
Nui Dinh
Nui Dat
Xuyen Moc
LONG AN
Can Duoc
Lang Phuoc Hoa
Hoa Long
Long Tan
Long Phuoc
Baria
Dat Do
Long Hai Hills
Long Phuoc Hai
Long Hai
Vung Tau
1 ALSG
Cap Saint Jaques
Go Cong
N
SOUTH CHINA SEA
0
25
KILOMETRES
CHINA
Hanoi
LAOS
Gulf of Tonkin
Mekong R.
Vientiane
THAILAND
Bangkok
CAMBODIA
Phnom Penh
Gulf of Siam
AREA ENLARGED
Saigon
SOUTH CHINA SEA
500 kms

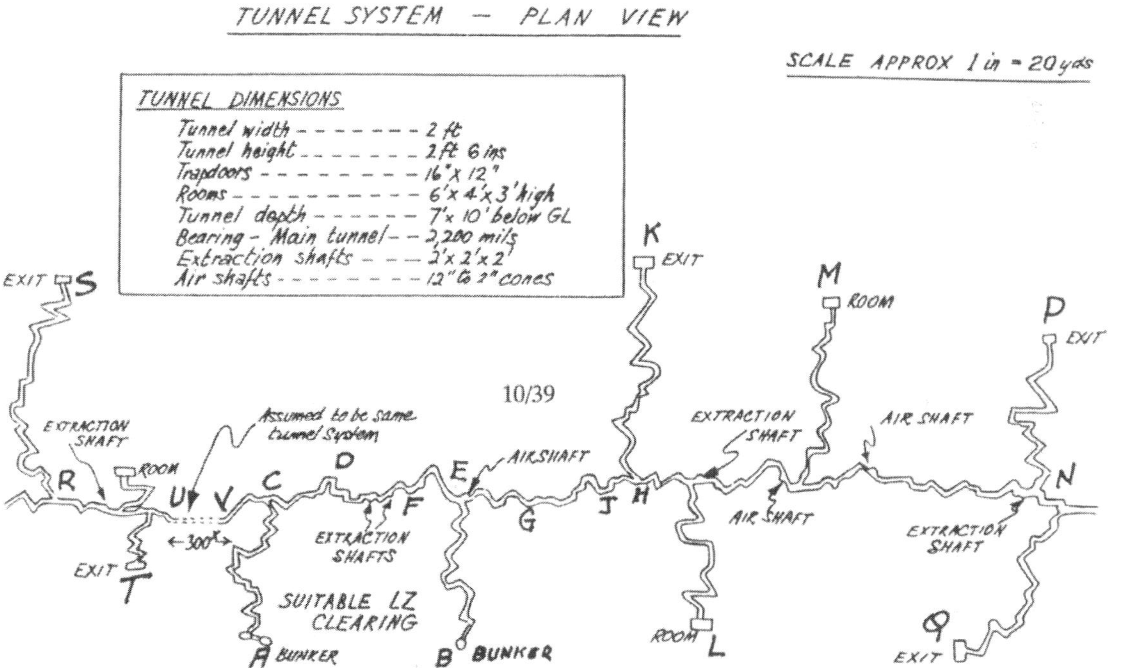


A plan of the Cu Chi Tunnels searched on 'Operation Crimp', January 1966. Four soldiers were killed or wounded from the enemy bunker at A. Engineers commenced their underground search from point A.

# PROLOGUE

## GOING UNDERGOUND

You launch yourself headfirst down a hole in the ground that's scarcely wide enough for your shoulders. After a couple of metres of slipping and wriggling straight down, the narrow tunnel takes a U-turn towards the surface, then twists again before heading off further than you can see with the battery-powered lamp attached to your cap.

Because the tunnel has recently been full of smoke and tear gas, you are wearing a gasmask. The eyepieces steam up and the sound of your own breathing competes with the thump of your heart to deafen you. You know you are not safe. You are in your enemy's domain and one of your comrades—a friend—has already died in a hole in the ground just like this one.

This is the stuff of nightmares: a tunnel that's almost too small to crawl along, dug by and for slightly built and wiry Vietnamese, not broad-backed Aussies or Americans.

Every inch forward has to be checked for booby traps, so you have a bayonet in one hand. Every corner could conceal an enemy soldier, perhaps one who can retreat no further, so you have a pistol in the other. There's no room to turn around. Going forward is difficult enough; backing out is nigh impossible. You know that the enemy knows you're there. You know your miner's light makes a perfect target. You switch it off. The silence is ominous, though not quite complete as the pounding of your heart throbs through your body. The velvet darkness is all-engulfing.

Then it becomes harder to catch your breath. You become light-headed, then dizzy and confused as the air runs out. Reason and sense evaporate as the darkness claims you. But you get a grip . . . you breathe . . . you bring it all back under control because the alternative—blind panic—means death. And you move on.

That's how it felt to be a Tunnel Rat. That's what it was like to know real fear—fear of being trapped, fear of an unseen enemy, fear of ever-present booby traps and, most of all, fear of the unknown. There was no military textbook, training class or official orders that told the diggers in 3 Field Troop who went down the Vietcong's tunnels what to expect and how to deal with it, for the very simple reason that they were the first. No Australian or American had ever explored a major tunnel system before.

On New Year's Day 1966, one of the most remarkable episodes in Australian military history began with a last-minute change of plan. The engineers of the newly formed 3 Field Troop had just been helping to free six armoured personnel carriers stuck in swamps near the Cambodian border. On their way back to camp, they were diverted to an area known as Ho Bo woods, north of Saigon, which was believed to contain the Southern Command headquarters of the Vietcong and North Vietnamese army. Intense Vietcong activity supported this theory but while carpet bombing of the area and intense artillery bombardments drove the enemy troops out, they seemed to reappear again soon after.

The Americans (and Australians, New Zealanders and Koreans) knew their South Vietnamese allies' HQ was riddled with Vietcong spies and assumed the Vietcong were getting advance warning of attacks, so that they could make themselves scarce. So they decided to order the launch of Operation Crimp in the field—a last-minute decision was taken to divert large numbers of troops to the area for a major search and destroy mission. It was called 'Crimp' because the American 173rd Brigade was to go through the north of the area while the Australians of the 1st Battalion, Royal

Australian Regiment (1 RAR) squeezed the enemy from the south.

But the day before the assault, 1 Battalion Operations Officer Major John Essex-Clark suspected, rightly, that they might be the ones caught in the jaws of a trap and demanded they switch to another landing zone. The suspiciously bare earth he had spotted in a reconnaissance flight would, indeed, turn out to be enemy defensive positions.

Even so, their 'hot insertion'—deployment by air under covering fire—met stiff resistance. The Australians were dodging bullets from the moment they hit the ground in their Huey helicopters. A signal from Saigon, warning the Vietcong that Crimp was on, was intercepted minutes before the first stick of choppers dropped onto the new landing zone.

This still didn't add up. The pounding the area had taken from artillery and air strikes should have cleared Vietcong forces before the ground troops went in. But they were still there and putting up one hell of a fight, popping up on all sides as the main wave of Aussie troops landed.

The Aussies were under constant sniper fire and skirmishes would break out as groups of Vietcong seemed to materialise out of thin air. Booby-trap bombs were going off, the diggers came under friendly fire from gunships who thought they were Vietcong, and their own artillery shells were creeping closer by the second.

It became apparent that the landing area Essex-Clark had

rejected would have been in the middle of a web of Vietcong crossfire that would have cut the Aussie troops to shreds. Even so, the Vietcong still had one trump card to play. When infantrymen tried to secure the clearing originally planned to be the landing zone, they discovered it was well defended with booby-trap bombs and spikes. When a couple of soldiers came under fire they dived into a washed-out gully beside a track and were shot at close range. Again, this didn't make sense. The area had been cleared and there shouldn't have been any enemy troops within range. When two medics crawled in to help the wounded, they too were both shot and killed.

That's when the Aussies realised the shots were coming from narrow slits in a mound of earth that looked no more threatening than an anthill. That deadly anthill would turn out to be the key to the Vietcong's secret weapon. The Aussies slept uneasily that night. They had discovered and neutralised the secret machine-gun posts but they could hear Vietnamese voices coming, it seemed, from the gates of hell below them. They didn't know they were right on top of their target—their enemy's command HQ was an underground city housing thousands of troops.

The following dawn, men from 3 Field Troop would blow that 'anthill' open and for the next week they and their comrades would go where no Westerner had gone before—down into the labyrinth of Vietcong tunnels that spread for kilometres in all directions and many metres into the bowels of the earth.

These weren't the first tunnels that American and Australian troops had encountered, but those they had come across previously had been short escape routes out from under huts and compounds. The standard procedure up to that point was to smoke out the inhabitants then blow up the entrances.

But the tunnels in Ho Bo Woods were no mere rat runs or boltholes. The Vietcong had set out to build underground cities with classrooms, hospitals and storerooms, and they had achieved their aim.

Had it not been for a bunch of larrikin Aussies who decided to explore the tunnels more thoroughly than anyone ever had before, that might never have been known. The men of 3 Field Troop went further than any Western troops had previously gone and in so doing became the original Tunnel Rats.

# 1. WHOSE WAR IS IT ANYWAY?

With the benefit of hindsight, the Vietnam War—from 1955 to 1975—was an inevitability. At the end of the Second World War, the political situation in Vietnam was precariously balanced between indigenous people who justifiably demanded the freedom to determine their own destinies and European powers who felt entitled to control their colonies. Under the rule of France, long before the war, control of Vietnam was passed around like an unwanted gift... to anyone but the Vietnamese themselves. It was also a pawn in a Cold War chess game in which the West's attitude to who should run the country was ABC—Anyone But Communists.

During the Second World War, the pro-Axis Vichy French government invited the Japanese to occupy the country.

Afterwards, when Vietnam was 'liberated' by the British, the local population demanded independence. This did not sit well with the Western powers and, incredibly, Japanese prisoners of war were freed and armed to help subdue local nationalists. The Potsdam treaty, in which the victorious Allies shared the world among themselves, saw Vietnam split between Chinese control of the north and British control in the south, but both soon withdrew and it was returned to French control.

The Vietnamese wanted freedom and they were ripe for revolution. Up to two million Vietnamese died in the north during a famine in 1945 caused largely by the French government's insistence that more land be given over to cash crops than food production. The charismatic Ho Chi Minh declared independence from France and encouraged the peasantry to rise up and loot the rice stores he believed had worsened the food shortages. A protracted war with France ended at the battle of Bien Dien Phu in March 1954 when an attempt to lure the Vietminh guerrilla forces into a conventional battle backfired. Instead of attacking the French, the Vietminh surrounded them and infiltrated their lines with the extensive use of tunnels while Vietminh reinforcements arrived from all over the country, building their forces up to about seven times that of the besieged French.

Facing defeat, France had asked America to intervene and even discussed the use of nuclear weapons against the

Vietminh, but US President Dwight Eisenhower wouldn't get directly involved unless their British allies were there too. Britain said they preferred to wait until meetings in Geneva, convened to also resolve the conflict in Korea, sorted out the future of the country.

Outthought and outfought, French troops were routed at Bien Dien Phu and France announced it was quitting Vietnam. In Geneva it was proposed that an independent Vietnam be divided into North and South, but no formal government be formed until after democratic elections in both parts. Ho Chi Minh believed, rightly, that he had enough support throughout the country to form a government in his own right but his Chinese backers pressured him into accepting partition.

The United States delegation proposed Ngo Dinh Diem as the new ruler of South Vietnam. The French argued against this, claiming that Diem was 'not only incapable but mad'. However, eventually it was decided that Diem presented the best opportunity to keep South Vietnam from falling under the control of communism.

Had there been free elections in both North and South, Ho Ch Minh would probably have won overwhelming support to lead a unified Vietnam. This view was shared by President Eisenhower. 'I have never talked or corresponded with a person knowledgeable in Indochinese affairs who did not agree that had elections been held at the time of the fighting, possibly 80 per cent of the population would have voted for the communist Ho Chi Minh,' he wrote later.

In any case, the despotic Diem refused to hold elections, saying the South (and America) had never signed an agreement. A devout Catholic in a predominantly Buddhist country, Diem embarked on a campaign of repression that saw tens of thousands imprisoned and executed. His targets were other religions and pro-communist political groups readying themselves for an election that would never take place. In fairness, the North also endured bloody purges but Diem's ruthless suppression of all possible dissenters and his promotion of Catholics in the government and army, regardless of their ability, had a whiff of the Borgias and the Spanish Inquisition rather than the excesses of Stalin and Mao.

Instead of elections, Diem staged a farcical referendum, run by his brother, that 'voted' against reunification by 98 per cent. Despite advice from American advisors not to over-egg the pudding, a miscalculation in the vote rigging meant Saigon voted 130 per cent in his favour.

So the North's National Front for the Liberation of Vietnam (better known in the West by the somewhat pejorative term 'Vietcong') began an insurrection in South Vietnam, targeting government symbols such as police, civil servants and teachers for assassination and infiltrating every level of government with spies and activists. Meanwhile, Diem continued to be an embarrassment to his American supporters but the 'domino theory'—that every time a country fell to communism, its neighbour would be under threat—convinced many Western leaders to stand by him regardless of his lunacies. This was a pattern America would repeat throughout Latin America where any government, no matter how corrupt, brutal or oppressive, was supported in preference to popular socialism.

The Cold War between Russia and the West was in full swing and American President John F. Kennedy had suffered the ignominy of the failed Bay of Pigs invasion in Cuba and the challenge of the Berlin Wall being built, so he felt he had to draw a line in the sand to protect America's status as leader of the free world and a bastion of democracy against the spread of communism. Vietnam, he decided, was where that line would be drawn.

But Kennedy did not want American troops to be fighting South Vietnam's war. Instead, like his predecessor President Eisenhower, he sent advisors to help train the South Vietnamese army (ARVN) in the hope they could withstand a growing insurrection themselves. But the ARVN was riddled with corruption and nepotism, with senior officers promoted on political and religious grounds and the troops focused more on deterring coups than fighting the North. The ARVN soldiers were brave and disciplined but their leaders were all too often weak, incompetent and corrupt.

With American involvement having increased from the initial allocation of 900 advisors sent by Eisenhower to 16,000 US personnel 'training' the ARVN, the US let it be known to disgruntled South Vietnamese military leaders that they wouldn't overreact if Diem and his brother were overthrown. There was a coup and they were both executed. Even so, Kennedy was still wary of direct military intervention and was actually pulling American advisors out when he was assassinated. His successor, Lyndon Johnson, had no such qualms. With a series of post-Diem military takeovers crippling the South Vietnamese leadership, the US military allegedly invented an attack on one of its own ships in the Gulf of Tonkin in 1962, so that Johnson could persuade the American Congress to give him permission to attack the North directly. America was now in a war in Vietnam, boots and all.

Back in Australia, Robert Menzies, the longest-serving Prime Minister in the country's history, had still to retire and the sixties had not even begun to swing for his country. Aborigines still didn't have the vote or citizenship (although they could fight for their country) but ten-pound Poms—Brits encouraged to emigrate to Australia by cheap passages—*could* vote and they didn't have to become Australian citizens to do so.

To right-wing Australians, old and new, the black and white rhetoric of the Cold War and the domino theory must have sounded like perfect sense. Few people had heard of

Vietnam and fewer still knew or cared where it was. Australia was still much more British than Asian and the public fear was that the Great Southern Land was too close to teeming third world countries for comfort. Also, Australia had obligations to America after the war in the Pacific and wouldn't turn its back on its allies.

America wanted it to seem that the South Vietnamese government wasn't a US puppet regime so they launched their 'many flags' policy of inviting other nations to fight alongside them. South Korea, for instance, sent more than 300,000 troops—six times the Australian commitment. Also, unlike Australian soldiers, American troops had little recent experience in jungle warfare, so the Australians' help was badly needed. At first, in 1962, there was a small force of 30, the Australian Army Training Team Vietnam, which by the end of 1964 had been joined by 200 Australian soldiers.

Late that year Prime Minister Menzies announced that there would be conscription for National Service and throughout 1965, in preparation for the arrival of National Service soldiers, regular Australian troops started arriving in Vietnam in significant numbers. Among them was the specially created 3 Field Troop, comprising 68 engineers drawn from ten serving engineer units, who were confronted with the full spectrum of engineering tasks, from dealing with booby traps to preparing the ground for the arrival of the first wave of conscripts.

Legend has it that when the army called for volunteers for 3 Field Troop, every serving engineer stepped forward. Why wouldn't they? They were regular soldiers, after all, and a trip to Vietnam would have seemed like an adventure. Then, according to 3 Field Troop lore, with more volunteers than vacancies, sergeants who'd been given the task of choosing who should go realised this was an opportunity to rid themselves of all the troublemakers in their units. Thus, the story goes, 3 Field Troop was made up of all the larrikins and ne'er-do-wells in the Australian Army's engineering ranks, brought together in one place.

This story is, of course, insulting to all the highly professional, responsible and committed soldiers who joined 3 Field Troop simply because they were the best men for the job. On the other hand, some of their colleagues turned out to be among the wildest bad boys ever to serve under the Australian flag, so the yarn has a tang of authenticity about it.

Back in Vietnam, the Americans were still struggling to get to grips with the complexity and magnitude of their task. 'We thought that we were going into another Korean War, but this was a different country,' General Maxwell Taylor, one of America's principal architects of the war, noted in hindsight. 'We didn't know our South Vietnamese allies and we knew less about North Vietnam. Who was Ho Chi Minh? Nobody really knew.'

They were beginning to discover that the South

Vietnamese ARVN was disorganised, demoralised and riddled with Vietcong sympathisers, so the South was never going to be able to effectively fight the war on its own. And while the North Vietnamese army, even though armed by China, could have been wiped out in a conventional war, the Vietcong, far from being the fanatical peasant rabble the propagandists would have had the West believe, were well organised, committed and unendingly resourceful.

Confronted by an enemy with overwhelming wealth, firepower and technology, they fell back on what they knew: their land and their people. Their heartfelt commitment to their cause and their use of booby traps, mines and especially tunnels made them impossible to beat.

The men of 3 Field Troop had to adapt very quickly to a form of warfare that not even they were prepared for. As engineers they were involved in construction of their facilities and destruction of the enemy's. One day they'd be dismantling booby traps and bombs, the next they might be building a bridge. But their basic training also made them much better equipped as jungle fighters than most of the Americans, who were expecting a different kind of war.

They were a different breed of soldier in a different kind of war and, one way or another, they were destined to make their mark on history.

# 2. A CONFLICT OVERSEAS

When 3 Field Troop was created, it was in response to a specific need. The Americans and the handful of Australians who had already seen action in Vietnam realised they were fighting a different kind of enemy. The Vietnamese had been fighting the French in a guerrilla war for decades and they had won. They were confident and competent.

So when a young captain called Sandy MacGregor was given his first active service command, he was provided with examples of booby traps, bombs and grenades that the first troops had encountered—obviously, the ones that hadn't gone off. As well as getting their basic training up to scratch, he had six weeks to knock the troop into shape.

The fact that they had been recruited from ten different

units exacerbated the problem and their default position was to form different cliques based on where they'd come from or where they might previously have served together. And then there's the simple fact that engineers are a breed apart in any army. Their unofficial motto 'Facimus et Frangimus' ('We make and we break') sums up their unconventional, almost bipolar approach to their jobs.

'Your average sapper is often not a pretty sight,' recalls Sandy. 'While the artillery and the tank corps might strut and preen in their razor-sharp uniforms and battle fatigues, the sapper is at his best in shorts and singlet and up to his elbows in mud.

'Engineering is a dirty job and a good engineer doesn't notice how filthy he gets while he's getting the job done. But that same scruffy soldier will also be the one who is called forward when the infantry spot a booby trap. He'll be the one who unfastens the tripwire and unscrews the detonator, asking himself if this bomb will be the one that is booby-trapped itself; or wondering if it's there to lure him into a sniper's sights.'

As he prepared 3 Field Troop, Sandy remembers there was a sense—and it may have been a feeling filtering down from senior officers—that they really didn't know what they could expect in Vietnam. There was also a belief that once the might of the Australian and American armies turned up on their doorsteps, the Vietcong would retreat to the north and, in that fateful phrase used in so many wars, they would all be home by Christmas.

'I trained them hard on booby traps, mines and explosives, but they still seemed to lack the conviction that they would even hear a battle, let alone be involved in one,' he says. 'Whatever it was, there was an air of unreality about their preparations.'

Six weeks is not a long time to build a combat troop from scratch and Sandy's task was made harder by the fact that the men were still arriving in dribs and drabs, some right up to the week before they were due to set sail. In the meantime, the troop would need to be virtually self-sufficient from the moment they set foot on Vietnamese soil and he had to organise everything from trucks to blankets.

Sandy MacGregor had tried everything in his power to get the troop working together, even sending them off on cross-country runs so that, if nothing else, they'd be unified in their hatred of him. But he wasn't there when they finally gelled as a unit—even if the fight was with their own side.

It was September 1965 when 3 Field Troop trudged up the gangplank of HMAS *Sydney*, a dilapidated aircraft carrier long overdue for decommissioning, en route for Vietnam. Sandy had flown ahead with Sergeant Gus Sant, to prepare the way while the rest of the troop followed by sea. It was on board the ship, when they were just a small number of men amid hundreds of others, that they started to show signs that they were coming together as a group.

They had been at sea for a few days when an announcement was made at the evening meal. The 105th Field Battery, Royal Australian Artillery, were on board and the gunners had decided to telegraph the Queen, their commander-in-chief, to inform her that they were on their way to Vietnam.

A reply had been received from the Palace and silence was demanded while one of the artillery officers read it aloud. 'From the office of Her Majesty, Queen Elizabeth II,' it said. 'Her Majesty has learned of your embarkation to join the conflict in Vietnam. She wishes you godspeed in your voyage, a successful completion of your mission and a safe return to your loved ones.'

The artillery blokes applauded, drowning out the hoots of derision from the other, less regally blessed units. Engineers and artillerymen are about as far apart as you can get in the Australian Army. The artillery see themselves as an elite, and award themselves the nickname the Nine-Mile Snipers. But to the larrikin engineers and other infantrymen, they are 'drop-shorts' who are supposed to fire over their own lines and into the enemy; any shells that land too close to their own front lines are going to generate a mixture of fear and anger.

As a result, the next night the parade was hushed when Staff Sergeant Laurie Hodge got to his feet and yelled: 'Could we have some quiet please. Three Field Troop has received the following telegraphic message, which I would now like to read out.'

A respectful if puzzled silence descended on the assembled troops, as Laurie pulled himself up, ready to address them. 'From Big Julie and Technicolour at the Railway Hotel. Bon voyage. Try not to get killed and we'll see you when you get back. Hope you don't mind if we screw your replacements while you're away! Cheers!'

The place erupted as 3 Field Troop, to a man, roared with laughter. Big Julie and Technicolour were what Sapper Keith Kermode called 'Railway Debs' at the troop's favourite drinking hole, the latter having earned her somewhat insensitive nickname from the large and vivid birthmark on her face. The gunners were furious and Laurie was whisked away by some officers. He didn't reappear for a couple of hours and never told anyone what was said to him but you can guess it was a lecture on respect for tradition . . . only at high volume and in colourful language.

The rest of the two-week voyage was spent with the troops reinforcing their basic training with exercises like target practice (shooting balloons off the back of the ship) and political indoctrination during which the padre explained the evils of communism, despite the fact that he was pretty much preaching to the converted. These were regular soldiers; half of them were already anti-communist and the other half didn't care if the enemy was red, green or blue. If the government said they were the enemy that was all they needed to know.

If the members of 3 Field Troop were expecting their landing at Vung Tau to be akin to the Normandy landings they had seen many times on film, they were about to be both relieved and disappointed. It was seven in the morning of 28 September 1965 when the *Sydney* dropped anchor off Vung Tau, about 130 kilometres south-east of Saigon.

The air was thick with expectation and Aussie accents but, as the sun's first rays lit Vung Tau beach—now a popular holiday resort—the Australian troops' anticipation gave it an air more reminiscent of Gallipoli than Bondi. First the soldiers had to clamber down rope ladders from the *Sydney*'s decks to the landing craft that bobbed below them. Then they surged towards the shore like the invading force they felt themselves to be.

Les Colmer remembered standing in the landing craft half expecting a volley of Vietcong bullets to spray them as they churned through the surf. They hit sand, the ramp crashed down, a whistle was blown and they charged . . . then jogged . . . then walked up the beach. Then they caught sight of their first Vietnamese—women and children selling Pepsi-Cola to the country's newest arrivals.

Bien Hoa, where the Australians would be based, is about 30 kilometres north-east of Saigon and is now a suburb of the renamed Ho Chi Minh City. It was only 150 clicks at most from Vung Tau but it had been decided to fly all the men, their essential stores and tents there. The rest was to be unloaded at the docks in Saigon and transported by road. The arrangements were a complete shambles and the units that were supposed to meet the troops and organise their transit to Bien Hoa didn't turn up.

Sandy MacGregor ended up organising the whole operation himself, even down to getting the stores loaded onto the transport planes. Even then, 3 Field Troop had to spend one night at Vung Tau while they found space on the transport planes to take them to Bien Hoa. And when they got there they discovered that their camp was no more than a clearing between the American lines and the bush. And it was pouring with rain.

Bien Hoa was the main air base in South Vietnam. The 173rd Airborne Brigade, comprising two American battalions and the Australian battalion (1 RAR), was given the dual task of defending the air base and of being the reaction force for an area that stretched from Cambodia in the west to the South China Sea in the east, and from Saigon in the south to Phuoc Long in the north. It was an area of about 25,000 square kilometres, slightly smaller than Wales in the UK and Maryland in the USA, and half the size of Tasmania.

Three Field Troop's base was 180 metres from the engineers of 173rd Airborne Brigade. It was a scrap of land smaller than two football pitches which had to accommodate 60-odd soldiers and all their earth-moving equipment.

They were billeted with the Americans for three days and got themselves set up in time, but only after working 18-hour days. Despite the chaos at Vung Tau, all their gear arrived, but they were lucky—other units lost whole pallets of stores.

'It was just a paddock of swamp, water everywhere, and we had to just build that into a camp,' says Mick McGrath. 'So you put your ammo boxes down, put your stretcher up between the ammo boxes, and Bob's your uncle. Except at Bien Hoa in the morning you'd still be wet because the ammo boxes just sink straight down into the quagmire.'

Les Colmer suffered worse than most because he was on picket duty on the first night. 'I just got there and they handed me my gun and told me I was on guard duty. By the time I was ready to set up my bivvy, all the good spots had been taken and I was down at the bottom where it was all mud.'

The Australians were understandably envious of the Americans' large dormitory tents. 'They were like big barrack rooms, when we only had four-man tents,' said Mick McGrath. 'It's a bit different if you've got 40 people all to pitch in and get one tent space ready. Out of the four people to put up our tent there'd be only two, because in that tent there might have been two of them out working. One thing about us was that we were always full-on at work. You had a job every day, whether it be mess duties, doing some road project, building a culvert, building a shower block or you were in the field.'

The Americans' hospitality to their new neighbours had

its limits, as became apparent at meal time. 'We lined up with our mess tins and the Americans had those ones with little scoops all over them, and we just had the old square dixies, you know, the big and the small,' recalled Sapper 'Sparrow' Christie, at 17 the youngest and the smallest of the troop. 'Mick Lee was lined up and some big boofhead of a Yank cook put a big ladle of custard all over his main meal for a joke. Mick just tipped it all out on the floor where he stood, went and washed his dixie and went and lined up again. There was custard and shit everywhere, and nobody said boo.'

The Americans were not, however, the enemy. They were out there in the jungle somewhere, dodging shells from artillery guns called Long Toms that were firing over the top of 3 Field Troop every hour, every night. It was called harassing and interdiction fire, had a range of about 15 to 17 kilometres and it was designed to keep the enemy on the move. The new arrivals didn't get much sleep for the first week until the booms became reassuring rather than disturbing.

The troop was given three weeks—until 20 October—to get their own camp ready and fully functional before they had to make themselves available to perform engineering tasks for other units. Even so, 1 RAR tried to get them working for them a week early and it took a message from the HQ of the Australian Armed Forces Vietnam to get them to back off.

When you're moving into virtually virgin territory the first thing you do is dig your weapons pits. They come before even tents since you won't need anywhere to sleep if you've just been overrun by the enemy. Because 3 Field Troop were now part of the perimeter of the main camp they had to be dug in and manned day and night from the first day. Later the machine-gun posts would be put in high towers overlooking the perimeter but digging the temporary pits in the torrential rain was a problem, as they kept filling up with water.

Next they had to establish their sections—3 Field Troop had three tents to a section, four men to a tent—and then they had to get their kitchen up and running, get their own stores in, dig latrines and start putting up their camp buildings. After that they started on basic facilities like toilets, which were just trenches or holes in the ground which they burnt out fairly frequently with diesel. Then, of course, there were the mess hall and the orderly room for the officers.

That's enough to be going on with at the best of times but because the ground was saturated, and it was a soggy, clay area, they had to put drains in. And until they put duckboards down, they had to wade through sticky mud. It took a long time for the ground to dry out, so the work was always a huge challenge. The troop also had to put up a workshop to service all the equipment—trucks, bulldozers, etc.—that they'd brought with them, and as the machinery bogged constantly they had to build tracks and roads as well as the drains they hoped would dry the land.

The troop had moved into an area which had been cleared as a kind of no-man's-land as part of the defences for the whole brigade. That way you can see the enemy crossing that last strip of land if they decide to attack you. With the new camp on the cleared land, the bush had to be cleared back another 100 metres on the other side of the wire to create a new safety zone. Three Field Troop had the equipment, the men and the skill to do all that and more, but soon discovered that there was a problem getting raw materials.

'If I had tried to go through the usual red tape to get what we needed I'd probably still be sitting in Bien Hoa waiting for it to arrive,' says Sandy MacGregor. 'This may sound ridiculous, but 1 RAR were on a very tight budget.'

Engineers are nothing if not resourceful, however, and they were lucky that they had their own transport as that meant they could acquire essential materials. For 'acquire' read steal from or trade with the Yanks. To the materials-starved Aussies, the Americans seemed to have mountains of everything, so when they needed timber, they took a couple of trucks down to the dock at Saigon and just loaded it up with a forklift that was sitting around nearby. Realising that they would need something to unload the timber at the other end, Sandy got his men to drive the fork-lift onto the back of the truck and took that too.

Mick McGrath, who was driving one of the trucks, says he was stopped at the gate by a South Vietnamese guard who asked him for some documentation. The only thing he had on him was the certificate they'd all been given when they crossed the equator on HMAS *Sydney*. But it looked official, had the Royal Australian Navy insignia on the top and the ARVN soldier on the gate could barely speak English, let alone read it, so they were allowed to pass. Pity help anyone who turned up after that who hadn't crossed the equator—their documentation would have looked second-rate compared with Mick's certificate.

The troop's first operation came only a week after they arrived and, rather than confronting them with the realities of jungle warfare, it left everyone wondering what all the fuss was about.

On 8 October, Sandy MacGregor and five NCOs went on their first mission as observers. He recalls their emotions were a mixture of fear and excitement but they were glad to get out of camp and into the field and away from the noise of the Long Toms. What a disappointment it turned out to be. Operation Ben Cat II in the Iron Triangle was a search-and-destroy mission into an area only 25 kilometres north of Saigon which was thought to have large Vietcong supply, maintenance and medical facilities and possibly two regiments hidden somewhere in the jungle.

The area had been pounded by B-52 bombers but it was

thought that the Vietcong had returned. In hindsight, it's almost certain that they had never actually gone away, since this was the area where 3 Field Troop later found the tunnel complex that made them famous. But with no idea that the Vietcong might be literally beneath their feet, this early operation was a non-event. They found a few booby traps and cleared a couple of villages. But they were all left with the feeling that if this was the war, they could handle it—the boredom was the worst of it.

Sandy MacGregor was in a very fortunate position for a young captain. Because he had to serve two masters—the Australians of 1 RAR and the Americans of the 173rd Airborne Brigade—it ironically meant he had more, rather than less, control over what he and his troop did. And since this was all new to everyone, he had a degree of autonomy unheard of for someone of his rank in the field.

That meant he could make sure 3 Field Troop were much more actively involved than engineers would normally have been. They all wanted to be in the thick of it and what they did to achieve that changed the way engineers operate to this day—and could have changed the course of the whole war.

# 3. THE FIRST TUNNELS

Whatever else you can say about engineers, they work hard. After the first month, two sections of 12 men each were sent out to do brigade work, while the rest stayed in the camp, half as the duty section—manning the machine-gun posts and other basic soldiering—and the others working on the camp itself. Those who went out to work for the brigade would be involved in everything from building shower blocks, kitchens and accommodation huts, mainly for 1 RAR, to clearing bush around the camp perimeter and fairly major civil engineering works. In that first couple of months the troop built ten helicopter pads, 2 kilometres of road and one small bridge.

They would then return to camp after a 10-hour day to

help with the work on their own projects, like proper toilets and showers and road works. Even when they'd been out on operations, that's what they'd be doing when other soldiers were sitting down to write letters. Sandy MacGregor was trying to get used to the fairly complex radio operating procedures, the codes and all the jargon. He had to keep up with all this so that he'd be ready when they were actually called into action.

Sandy tried to train his batman, Les Colmer, on all the codes and map reading, so that he could keep things moving if Sandy was killed or wounded. Sandy always had the utmost faith in Les, although he discovered years later that his faith was slightly misplaced—Les used to mug his way through.

'Most of it was over my head,' said Les, years later. 'I didn't even know where the bloody Cambodian border was. If you showed me a map I'd say "Yeah" but you couldn't sit me in the jungle and expect me to say "Oh, it's over there, four clicks that way." But it didn't worry me. I just drew up some notes and they'd give us the general direction. My main worry was how many thousand yards we were going to do a day.

'Basically, I bullshitted. I just faked it. Sandy used to carry his own map and I used to carry mine and sometimes he'd give me directions and I'd go and tell Laurie Hodge where we were going and how many men we needed. I just sort of played along with it and tried to keep the job.

'I wasn't very good at radio work, either. I remember the first time I used the radio over there we were going on a big operation and I couldn't remember Sandy's codename. So I just said, "Is Captain MacGregor there?" and the next thing they were screaming and yelling. I was supposed to say "Is Sunray Holdfast there?" (Sunray = boss; Holdfast = engineer) I had a lot of trouble.'

The first operation in which 3 Field Troop played an active role began on 23 October and was called War Zone D. The battalion was on a basic search-and-destroy mission. It was only going to take three days and they went along to help with the repair and maintenance of any bridges along the way, to prepare landing zones and gun areas and to demolish any tunnels or enemy installations they might find. This was their motto—'We make and we break'—brought to life.

There were 17 on that mission and they were kept busy, although there were no great dramas. Most of the time they were classifying bridges to work out what sort of weight could go over them, in preparation for a bigger operation planned for a later date where some heavy machinery was going to be moved around. HQ needed to know an armoured personnel carrier wasn't going to collapse a bridge halfway across. Leaving aside that specific problem, they would also be creating a bottleneck of men and equipment that would be a sitting target for the enemy. The engineers also had to classify roads in much the same way, for the same reasons.

However, one day they found some tunnels, which got everyone excited. Sandy remembers being called forward and standing there thinking, 'There's the tunnel, boys . . . what do we do now? We'd heard about the Vietcong tunnels all over Vietnam but up to that point none of 3 Field Troop had actually seen one. They didn't know what to expect and weren't quite sure what to do.

'But I did know that I wanted to find out what was down there and I wasn't prepared to ask the men to do something I wouldn't do myself,' recalls Sandy. 'So, just in case the boys needed to haul me out again, I got one of the blokes to tie a rope round my ankles and then they lowered me head-first into the hole, with a torch in one hand and a bayonet in the other. I was let down the tunnel with a guy after me and I didn't know what to expect.

'All I could do was prod the earth with my bayonet and shine the light to see if I could find anything. It doesn't matter how small the tunnel is—you never know where it's going to turn around, you don't know what's around the bend. You don't know what's in the floor, you don't know if it's abandoned, you don't know if it's booby-trapped and you don't know why the tunnel is there in the first place.'

More often than not, a tunnel was just an escape run from underneath a house, ending up in a storm drain or a nearby rice paddy. This first tunnel ended less than 10 metres away inside a house which they had already searched. But the area was not occupied by Vietcong, so there was nothing terribly sinister about it, and Sandy got all his men to go through the tunnel one by one, to see what it was like. Later on they found another tunnel entrance down a well, and then were able then to figure out that there was a network of open trenches which ran into tunnels, some of which had little rooms off them. From that they deduced that the tunnels were either for personal protection or were escape routes. Most of them were not booby-trapped, some were not even hidden and many of them were open.

Les Colmer, who was also the troop's unofficial photographer, took a picture of Sandy's boots protruding from the tunnel with the rope round his ankles. The picture was sent back to Australia where it eventually became *Pix* magazine's 'Pic of the Week'. The powers that be in the army were horrified to see that a troop commander was going down tunnels. Sandy received a polite but firm directive from Brigadier Jackson, 1 RAR's commander in Saigon, that tunnel clearance was not a job for captains and he was expected to stay above ground.

Back in camp, life began to get a bit more tolerable. Using a little engineering ingenuity, the troop built their own hot-water system, which was very clever but, at the same time, very simple. You run a pipe under your hot-water tank from your diesel supply. You bend it back under itself and drill a few holes in the top side of the bottom section of pipe. Once it's lit, as well as warming the water, the flame heats the section of pipe above it, which turns the diesel into gas, which makes the heater work even more efficiently.

Now that they had hot and cold running water, they needed to build proper showers (rather than sprinkler roses attached directly to gravity feeds). And for proper showers they needed bathroom fittings that the army would not have provided even if they hadn't been cash-strapped. The money, it was decided, would come from the troop's casino. Originally just a corner of the mess tent that was given over to the odd game of cards, two-up and crown and anchor, the casino came into its own with the arrival of the troop's mess hall.

Since the 1 RAR ration was two beers per man per day, it was not deemed necessary to give 3 Field Troop a separate 'wet' mess where supplies of alcohol could be locked away safely. But since they served two masters, Sandy didn't see why they shouldn't choose the more advantageous of the two, in terms of alcohol supplies. And since the army had supplied a nice, prefabricated, secure mess hut, he didn't see why they shouldn't stick to the mess tent they already had and put the new hut to much better use. So the mess hut was built in a hollow by the bend of a stream, a poker machine was leased from army supplies in Saigon and alcohol was bought very cheaply from their American comrades.

The profits went into making the troop's camp one of the best equipped in Vietnam, with many other 'luxuries', like electric cable, 3-point plugs, chairs and, later on, spare parts that they couldn't get from the resupply system, all bought with the casino's profits. These guys didn't miss a trick.

'Sandy found this Yank supplies depot on the road to Saigon and they had this weird thing that if one can in a carton of beers had burst, they'd throw the whole case out,' recalls Sapper Keith Kermode, one of the troop's drivers. 'For a few dollars you could just load the back of the truck up from this mountain of burst boxes. And there was never more than one or two bad cans in a case.'

The casino became a popular haunt for the men, and not only from 3 Field Troop. Soldiers from other units would slip through the wire to drink with them, and Americans—especially the African-Americans—became frequent visitors, despite the fact that they had their own, much fancier casino.

'They had poker machines and a big swimming pool,' recalls Mick Lee. 'They used to love the Australians because a thing called "the grip" was all the rage then. Some Australian mob had gone to Las Vegas. They had a certain way of pulling the handle and ended up getting barred. Being Aussies, we used to say we knew the grip and, lo and behold, we used to pull these jackpots off. But it was only sheer luck; we didn't really know what we were doing.'

You would have thought being allowed to have their own

unofficial wet mess would have been enough, but no. After the bar had been locked up for the night, the men would tunnel their way under the boards and pass the beer out, even if, to their credit, they always left the money. But their casual drinking wasn't without its consequences.

'I was coming past the American camp one day,' recalls Keith Kermode, 'and this guy comes out and says, "Hey, buddy. Do you know what's happened to our water?" The Yanks took their water supply from the stream that ran past our casino, so I had a fair idea. I walked back up the stream and there, just inside our boundary, was the answer. The stream was blocked with beer cans—when we were drinking on the sly, we used to just throw them in the water and they'd kind of built up.

'So I went back down and told the Yank that I thought I knew what the problem was and I'd have it fixed in no time. I raced back into the camp and me and a couple of the others cleared the dam. That Yank probably still thinks I'm a great engineer.'

Apart from hot water, the other great necessity of modern life is electricity. Three Field Troop had to go without for the first few weeks, until they came across an American depot for broken-down equipment, in the middle of which was a huge diesel-driven generator, rated at 30 kVA—that's a lot of electricity. They weren't allowed to cannibalise one piece of equipment to fix another, but they were allowed to take anything broken down that they could fix . . . and 3 Field Troop had someone who could fix anything.

'Waxy' Rayner was on detachment to the troop from the Royal Australian Electrical and Mechanical Engineers (RAEME) and there wasn't a machine made that he couldn't repair. The men used to take him their watches—this was before digital watches and microchips—and he'd have them working in no time. Corporal Rod Goater, who was the RAEME detachment commander, helped to get the engine going and Waxy worked out that it would be fine as long as they didn't stop it. He then devised a way of doing a complete oil change while the generator was still running, which meant it never stopped from the day he got it going to the day it blew itself to oblivion . . . but that's another story.

That generator was nicknamed Buddha—it was driven by a Buda-Lanova engine—and became something of a mascot for the troop. Buddha was spitting out enough power to light the whole air base, let alone 3 Field Troop's corner, but it served another purpose too. 'We used to have little seats all around there, it was like a little garden setting,' says Mick Lee. 'We'd sit around and sing and yell out and talk and crack jokes and the noise from Buddha used to drown it all out.'

Three Field Troop's other mascot was the dog, Smedley. And he too provided entertainment for the lads. Every so often the men would capture rats and, when they got a break, they'd put the rats and Smedley inside a huge water tank then take bets on how long it took him to kill them. It would be considered cruel today but in the middle of a war zone where human lives were lost on a daily basis, it seemed like harmless enough fun.

On 5 November, Sandy MacGregor led a small detachment of 16 men on Operation Hump, which took them to an area slightly north of where they'd been during the previous mission. Again, it was a basic search-and-destroy operation, with the focus on any villages they might find. It must have been around this time, he recalls, that he began to realise that the army wasn't as well organised as it might have been.

They had been told that once they had been dropped off by helicopter, they should rendezvous with B Company's headquarters staff, who would tell them where they should be deployed. But when they got there, B Company weren't where they were supposed to be and they wasted a lot of time chasing after them.

When they did finally find out where to go, they were called forward to help search a village. It turned out that, firstly, the village was abandoned and, secondly, B Company hadn't given the troop enough time to complete the search and they had to be pulled out anyway. The policy at that time was that all areas under military control had to be cleared of civilians. The reason for that was that civilians would, willingly or unwillingly, hide Vietcong fighters. The local population was relocated and rehoused in safe areas and, in fact, 3 Field Troop did a lot of work building houses and establishing services for relocated Vietnamese civilians. The reasoning was that the locals were being protected from the Vietcong (which they were, in a way) but they were also being protected from what happened next. After an area was cleared in that way, anyone in it who wasn't in the army was deemed to be the enemy.

The reason engineers were being used for searches was that even an abandoned village could be full of hidden dangers. Every door or cupboard or tunnel entrance could conceal a booby trap. It wasn't very clever to go crashing around knocking doors down like they do in the movies. The Vietcong even devised a special booby trap for door-kickers. It was two panels of spikes, hinged in the middle and hung inside the door. Anyone who smashed through a door might stop before the first, upper panel got them, but then the lower flap would swing through and spike them from waist to knee.

With that kind of fiendish trap round any corner, the army preferred to have engineers painstakingly check everything while the infantry boys watched their backs.

The village in question was called Xom Cay Xoai and consisted of about 150 huts and small buildings. Almost all the huts had some form of air-raid shelter or bunker, either inside or attached to the outside. The troop went back to it the next day and some documents, clothes, magazines and booby-trap switches were found, suggesting that Vietcong troops had at least passed through. They also found about 20 tunnels between 2 and 5 metres long, and two bigger ones—6 and 10.5 metres long—which they demolished, according to standard procedures.

The next day they were supposed to be resupplied with explosives so they could demolish two 10-metre wells. But the helicopter carrying the explosives didn't arrive until too late and they didn't have enough time to do the job properly. They finished off the job the next day and on the day after that—the final day—they blew up a few mortar blinds. Then the choppers arrived to take the engineers, including a somewhat disillusioned Sandy MacGregor, back to camp.

'I was beginning to realise that we were pretty much feeling our way in these operations and it was up to me to make sure anyone who came after us didn't make the same mistakes or suffer similar delays to us,' he recalls. 'Because of that, my reports began to be quite specific about what should and should not be done.'

Sandy felt 3 Field Troop were lucky in being allowed to learn gradually about the challenges that confronted them. They were being eased into this new kind of warfare rather than being dropped into the middle of it. And one of his reports was incredibly prescient in a suggestion he had about the tunnels.

'It is felt that if any tunnels in a relatively friendly area are known to exist then very valuable experience would be gained by the troop practising searching, employing the use of tear gas,' he wrote. In the end, he got the troop to build their own tunnel to practise in and to this day believes the only reason they had to do this themselves was because no American or Australian had ever gone down the tunnels before.

# 4. THE AIRBORNE AMERICANS

Australian soldiers, many of whom had the somewhat cynical British perspective on American troops, didn't relish the thought of fighting alongside US soldiers. However, once they did, their opinions changed. 'The Americans were different, sure. But they weren't inferior,' says Sandy. 'I don't think I've ever seen more bravery than was displayed by the men of E Troop 17 Cavalry Regiment.'

This modern version of the cavalry had jeeps instead of horses and 50-calibre machine guns mounted on the back, instead of sabres and pistols. They were so comparatively lightly armed because they had to be movable by air and quick on the ground when they were dropped in. Each jeep had a crew of four: the gunner, his offsider who fed the ammunition, a radio operator and a driver. If the gunner got shot—and there was no protection—the man feeding the ammo belt took over, and everyone moved up. If he got shot, the radio man took over, and so on until they'd all been taken out.

'I remember once going out with a mob with the jeeps and the 50-cal machine gun and I felt so unprotected,' said Sandy Saunders. 'I'd rather be walking along in the bush than sitting up in those things with no protection. They're just a duck-shooting target as far as I'm concerned. I think their officers were trying to win more battle colours—I don't think the diggers were. There might have been a few nuts, but they're humans those people too, you know. I felt sorry for them poor buggers just standing up there with just a 50-calibre. He'd be the first bloke you'd shoot. They always go for the bloke on the gun and it only takes one shot because there's no protection.'

The essential difference between the Australian soldier and the American in Vietnam was that the Aussies used stealth where the Americans used firepower. That's why, when the engineers were on attachment to American troops, they'd often be used as forward scouts. They didn't like being sent to work with the US troops all that much but if it was an engineering task, they did it. If the Americans needed a particular piece of equipment, like the Oliver dozer and backhoe or front-end loader, they would take an operator and a truck driver out with them. The engineers weren't supposed to be with them as field soldiers, supporting infantry; they were there to operate the equipment and maybe delouse booby traps.

The American engineers had the same financial and logistical support as their infantry: where the Australians often had to improvise with whatever they had to hand, the US forces would have men, equipment and raw materials in abundance. In Operation Rolling Stone (described in detail later in the book) they could build 2 kilometres of road a day through the jungle. But their tactics left the Aussies who fought alongside them bewildered.

'I found Americans to be brave at times to the point of being ridiculous, generous to a fault and, probably the same way they find Australians, brash, uncouth and several other things,' says Snow Wilson. 'They were exceptionally nice people but I could never bring myself to operate the way they did. We have all probably seen a few movies about Vietnam and seen these guys with transistors hanging round their neck and the camera hanging below that and a cigar hanging out of their mouth and a couple of socks hanging off their basic webbing with tins in. That was exactly how they were. I couldn't believe it!'

Les Colmer felt quite comfortable with the Americans' 'informal' approach.

'I found it pretty slack but it suited the engineers' way

of life,' said Les. 'It didn't suit the infantrymen, though. But there was nothing wrong with their fighting ability. They fought like demons and died like bloody heroes. But the infantry used to complain about being with Americans because they just sort of blundered through, as if they're saying "Here we are—come and get us."

'In fact it was an American tactic to make a noise, attract enemy fire and then give the enemy every bit of hardware that they could muster. But the Australian way was to almost fight like the Vietcong did, stay concealed, stake 'em out. I read somewhere about a fire support base with mortars, artillery, tanks and about 500 men. It was a blocking force and the Vietcong would come down there every night and have a go at them. So the Yank commander said to the Aussies, "You patrol my perimeter at night and I'll fight the Vietcong during the day . . . You keep them out, 'cause you're best at it."'

One of the most significant differences between the two armies' daily routines was their 'clearing' procedure at night. The Australians would send a patrol out from each machine-gun post to the farthest point at which they could still see the compound wire and each other. Then, as they returned—and always to the next gun-post so they would be recognised—each man would call out his name, adding 'with two behind' or however many men were yet to return, and so on. The machine gunner would then know that anybody who was out there after the last man came in was almost certainly enemy.

The Americans, on the other hand, used to 'clear by fire'—in other words, blast away into the jungle for a few minutes every night and morning. The Aussies considered this not only wasteful and inefficient—it doesn't take too much imagination to hide in a ditch or behind a tree—but downright dangerous. More than once they'd have men out on patrol when the Americans opened up and on at least one occasion their shots were coming right through jungle to where 3 Field Troop were camped at the other side.

Mick McGrath, who spent six weeks on attachment with American forces, has mixed but generally fond memories of the US troops: 'The Americans had the utmost admiration for us and we heard that the American brass wished they'd had more Australians over there. No matter where you went, they seemed to welcome you with open arms.

'On the social side, the Yanks have always got something to sell and they aren't always real good bargain hunters. I was told before I went not to worry about taking any clothes—just a kit bag full of slouch hats and badges and things and worry about getting restocked with a uniform when I got over there. I wish I had, because I could have bought all the uniforms I wanted to for the rest of my life. I once got a brand-new pair of boots for a rag hat and you could never compare the value of the two.'

But it wasn't all trade and barter. Mick spent a lot of time in the field with the Americans and found that when they said 'Come and get us', the Vietcong didn't have to be asked twice.

'Wilfie Eyles, Geoff (Beau) Guest and I were attached to the 173rd Airborne Brigade,' recalls Mick. 'I had Wilfie's Oliver backhoe on the back of my tipper, Beau had the TD-15 dozer on the back of a Yankee low-loader and we were away with them for six weeks straight. It was good experience but it was pretty harrowing at times. The Vietcong sometimes didn't seem to want to fight us Australians at all. Even when they had a chance, a lot of times they'd go without firing a shot. But they never missed a chance to have a shot at or antagonise the Yanks. On other operations when I was with Australians they would sort of torment us or let us know they were there without actually trying to engage us, it seemed to me.'

The men from 1 RAR and 3 Field Troop who were ambushed and fired on in operations like Crimp and Silver City would disagree, but Mick's view does help point out a difference in attitudes.

'I think they were wary of the Australians because we don't just sort of stand and blaze away,' says Mick. 'We'll try and encircle the enemy and get 'em. The Yanks would sit back and just shoot, shoot, shoot until they got their kill and make a lot of noise doing it, but we'd been taught differently.

'On that operation, Wilf and Beau and I could never get used to the American's idea of "stand to". They used to clear their front by fire of a morning to just warm up their weapons for the day. But the Yank that was driving the low-loader and us three Aussies kept ourselves pretty well to ourselves. We made sure we were safe every night, as safe as we could make ourselves, by camping underneath the low-loader. Where it wasn't practical to do that, the dozer would come off, dig a big enough scrape for the four of us to get in and we'd position the equipment so that we had protection.

'During the day we still ran our own race. They were building this part of the road and they had Yank trucks belting up and down the highway. I must have looked like the proverbial pimple on the elephant's arse, with my little tipper trying to keep up with them. But they seemed to appreciate me there working alongside them.

'Anyway, one day we got hit with sniper fire and the convoy stopped and I just sort of pulled up alongside of everybody else and watched the little show down the road. There was a mob of Yanks all hiding behind rubber trees firing odd shots. Then the word came down, and they brought up this recoilless rifle mounted on the back of a one-and-a-half-tonner. It's a 105mm gun—more like a small cannon than a big rifle—and they used it to blow the top out of every tree they saw until they stopped the sniper. You'd pay big dollars to go and see it now.'

Later, the patrol came to a section of road where the Vietcong had come in during the night and chopped all the road up to make it impassable. So they asked Beau Guest to take the TD-15 off the low-loader and fill in all the holes with the dozer. Wilf and Mick cut through the bush and went further down the track to where there was plenty of earth in the banks at the side of the track, and worked back towards the dozer, filling the holes.

'So Wilfie takes the loader off and I'm just sort of standing there and a bloke comes up the road on a pushbike and Wilfie, who was backing up, looked over his shoulder and saw me give the bloke a smack up the side of his head with my rifle butt,' says Mick. 'Wilf stopped the loader and jumped off and says "What did you do that for?" and I said "He's got grenades in this fruit"—you could see where they were cut to hide the grenades. So the Vietnamese was in a bit of a flat spin on the side of the road and we tied him up and that's when the Yanks got brave and followed my wheel tracks through the scrub.

'Anyway, this colonel pulls up in this jeep and I said, "I caught this silly bastard here coming down the road on that pushbike there and he's got grenades in the fruit." So he got on the radio and he said, "The Australians have cleared the road to my position, we are now going to proceed." By this time there's about half a dozen vehicles had pulled up behind him and they had a couple of those 13 hundredweight utes with all the sandbags and machine guns and everything all bristling.'

The American convoy had only gone 40 metres when the Vietcong set off a mine. They let the jeep with the officer through and another jeep with a machine gun on it pass, then detonated as the truck bristling with guns passed.

'The blast just picked it up and flipped it right over and all you could hear was people screaming,' recalls Mick. 'Then Charlie [the Vietcong] opened up from the scrub. So I told Wilf to look after the bloke we'd captured and I'd go and see how Beau was. I ran down there, because I was protected by this big bank that we were going to dig out of, and there's Guestie still working away with the dozer. He couldn't hear a thing because he had his earmuffs on.

'There were bullets screaming around the place everywhere and I'm waving, trying to draw his attention and throwing rocks at the dozer. Then he looked up and took the earmuffs off and heard it all. He nearly shit himself. It was funny, even though it was pretty serious at the time. Anyway, Wilfie and I found a safe spot behind this bank and watched the Yanks really putting it on the Vietcong. They didn't hesitate to call the planes in and two of them arrived, just strafing, and this other one that came in later had the two big napalm bombs underneath.

'So I said to Wilf, "Have a look at this, this'll be a good one." Anyway, as he came in he's dropped the first one and its nose snagged and the tail went sideways. So, when he dropped the second one, the nose of the second one hit the tail of the first one and dislodged it. But the jolt ignited the second bomb and these two napalm bombs just exploded right above our heads. It was just like a gigantic thunder clap and our ears just screamed and we couldn't breathe 'cause there was no air.

'Just about the same time this little Vietcong had started to come to after I'd given him the tap. He looked up but he couldn't breathe—he must have thought he was dead. I looked at Wilfie and he was struggling but it passed pretty quick and we were all right. But I'll never forget the look of terror on that little bloke's face.'

The American troops grew to respect the Australians' capabilities as jungle fighters, occasionally—as has been mentioned—using them as forward scouts, and in one case when there were no engineering jobs to do, forming the sappers into an extra infantry patrol. For Sandy Saunders, being stuck out in front was preferable to being tail-end Charlie when the Americans had already gone crashing through the jungle.

'I remember on one operation I was on an ambush patrol by night and this Vietcong force that intended to attack a Yankee engineering unit stumbled into us. The Vietcong didn't know we were in front of them. They were just getting ready to prepare to line up to attack the Americans and then we opened up on them. We had a completely different system to the Americans and that must have confused them.

'The Yanks acted as if they were still fighting in Europe, whereas we were jungle trained. Most of our tactics came out of New Guinea, Malaya and Borneo, so it was just what we'd been doing for years. The tactics weren't any different as far as we were concerned,' he said. 'I didn't mind it when they used us as forward scouts. I'd rather be up there on our own rather than back with the bulk of them with their noise.'

For all these joint missions and secondments, most of the men in 3 Field Troop had closer contacts with the Americans socially than they did in the field. Their little casino—with its cheap beer and 'strange' gambling games like two-up and crown and anchor—was a real magnet to the Americans. That was especially true of the African-Americans, who found the Aussies a lot less racist than many of their own white comrades. It was a situation that Sparrow Christie exploited to the full.

'I used to go over the wire into the American compound where the sergeant that used to run the workshop was a big black guy called Crow. I guess because my nickname was Sparrow, I got on all right with him. He got me an American uniform and I'd slip over to him, dress up in it and drive his jeep into town.'

Sparrow and Crow were obviously not authorised to go anywhere, together or alone. But the guards on the gate would always assume that Crow was an officer, simply because he was being driven around in a jeep.

'When we used to pull up at the Provos [short for Provost Marshalls] he'd poke shit at me being a white man driving a blackfella around and we'd get through,' says Sparrow. 'But I couldn't drink too much because I had to drive back. So we'd go and get our rocks off, come back and then I'd just drink his booze in his fridge. He had everything in that workshop.'

Americans and Australians were natural allies, and fought well together, despite their differences. Judging by the way Sparrow and Crow conspired to get to the brothels of Bien Hoa, they played together pretty well too, with the difference in the colour of their skins being an asset rather than an issue.

# 5. TROOPING THE COLOUR

Three members of 3 Field Troop weren't even Australian citizens. They weren't American or Vietnamese advisors, or even New Zealanders strengthening the old Anzac ties. They were two Aboriginal men and a Thursday Islander and, shocking as it may seem now, it wouldn't be until two years after the troop was formed that Aborigines and Torres Strait Islanders were granted full Australian citizenship.

'Bill Unmeopa, Billy Coolburra and Dave Cook were, in very different ways, great assets to the troop,' says Sandy MacGregor. 'And, you may be surprised to learn, they were rarely, if ever, subjected to racism. The strong bond between soldiers—and engineers in particular—transcended more obvious differences like colour and culture.'

'Being so close together and so far from home, we didn't have anyone else to turn to except each other,' said Billy Coolburra, referring to the other members of the troop, not just the other Aboriginal men. 'Obviously I knew we were from different backgrounds. They used to dish it out to me and I'd dish it out to them. It was in fun. When it came to looking after each other it didn't matter if you were black or white. It's not the colour of your skin that makes the man, it's what's in your heart.'

That view wasn't always shared by the American Allies. 'There was a bit of racism there,' said Billy. 'I remember there was an argument broke out with the guys of 173 Brigade engineers, they were American, and I got between them and said "Come on, fellas, we're here to fight the Vietcong, not each other." And this bloke came up to me and said I had a funny accent and asked where I was from. I told him I was a full-blood Aboriginal and I said we should be making friends because we never knew when we would have to depend on each other. The next night we all got together and sang songs together and started talking about our homes. We made a lot of friends—it was good.'

Billy's good nature and diplomatic skills often saw him called on to act as a mediator between the black and white Americans. Certainly, a lot of the black soldiers found it easier to socialise with the Australians than with their white comrades—no doubt due in part to the fact that they were from the Southern states where the civil rights movement was only just starting to make an impression.

'Billy was worth his weight just as a morale booster for the troops,' says Sandy. 'He could play the guitar and sing and would give everybody's spirits a lift just by being around. He was also a bloody good soldier—if you could get him to keep his boots on. He never once let me down when we were on an operation, but back at camp he'd often just disappear into the bush—always barefoot—and would not return until long after he was posted as absent without leave.

'I think the Australian Government saved a fortune on Billy's wages, the number of times he was given "14 and 14", 14 days confined to barracks, 14 days loss of pay. But I wouldn't have dreamed of sending him home—he was just too valuable to us.'

The troop almost lost Billy permanently a couple of times, the first being on Operation New Life, when he was carrying the M-60 heavy machine gun in a patrol that was clearing the area round a rice paddy.

'What the Vietcong usually did was to pick off either the forward scout, the officer, the radio man or the man with the firepower. That was me,' explains Billy. 'Fortunately, I am left-handed, which causes a few problems with the M-60. However, on this occasion it probably saved my life. I had just lifted the gun to adjust it and was holding it across my chest when a sniper fired at me. Lucky for me, the bullet hit the gun and ricocheted away.'

Billy lost another of his nine lives in March 1966, on Operation Silver City. The troop was sent out to a place near the Cambodian border where there were large caches of rice and salt that either had to be retrieved or destroyed before they fell into Vietcong hands. Billy and John 'Tex' Cotter were called in to 'delouse' a pile of rice bags.

'The bags were on platforms and they were stacked about eight feet high,' Billy recalls. 'They were stacked in such a way that if you moved one, the others would fall over. They were obviously booby-trapped. And all the time the infantry boys were telling us to hurry up because there were about 2000 Vietcong heading in our direction. That's when the cache went up with me and Tex on top of it. We were lucky because the main force of the blast was in between us and the rice bags absorbed most of it. As it was, they said I was blown 20 feet in the air. I had the wind knocked out of me and Tex got some shrapnel in the side of his eye. We were lucky too that none of the other grenades went off. We must have taken about 24 grenades out of that stack, all wired together so that if you moved certain bags, the whole lot would go off.'

One of Billy's best friends in camp was 'Snow' Wilson, whose hair was as white and whose skin was as pale as Billy's were black. The two were great mates and were known as 'the twins', which used to confuse outsiders when they were introduced to them. One night in Saigon, Billy and Snow were drinking in a bar when they got into a fight with some American Green Berets.

'One of them pulled a pistol so I hit him with a chair. Then Snow got hit from the other side, and he hit him back, then the American Shore Patrol came so we ran out the back,' Billy recalls. There, with its engine running, was a three-wheeled Lambretta taxi—like a Bangkok tuk-tuk—which Snow and Billy commandeered.

'We took off but the Shore Patrol followed and started shooting at us,' Billy recalls. 'Snow was driving and he took us down one-way streets, and drove on the wrong side of the road—anything to get away from them. We drove all the way from Saigon to Bien Hoa, dodging in and out of traffic, with more and more people chasing us as we went along. First it was the Shore Patrol, then the Australian MPs, then the Vietnamese MPs, then the White Mice [Vietnamese civilian police] and at the end the Airport Police joined in too.

'By the time we got to the camp at Bien Hoa, they had just about caught up with us. Then we noticed the boom gate was down. I shouted to Snow "What are we going to do?" and he just said "Get your head down!" We went straight under the boom, jumped off the Lambretta and ran into the camp.'

With half the military police in South Vietnam baying for Australian blood, Sandy MacGregor did what a team player does and told them he'd deal with it himself, collared Billy and Snow, gave them a dressing-down and confined them to barracks for a week.

'As far as I was concerned, the only thing that mattered was that they had made it back to camp before curfew,' he says. 'And I didn't really care who they brought with them and how they'd got there. I certainly couldn't afford to have two good men locked up—we were short-handed as it was.'

Snowy and Billy truly were the terrible twins—inside, if not on the surface—and their fame reached high places.

'I was down at the American RAP [regimental aid post] in Vung Tau one day seeing what was wrong with me,' recalls Snow. 'And MacGregor and Hodge came screaming up in our old Willys jeep saying "Get in, get in!" I said I hadn't even seen the bloody medic but they just told me to get in the jeep. So they raced me back to camp, issued a brand-new uniform, brand-new boots, and there's MacGregor ironing me a shirt, and a new pair of trousers. He told me to go and clean my belt and boots.

'So I says, "OK, but would somebody tell me what's going on?" "You're going for lunch with the Prime Minister," says Sandy and I said "What the fuck am I going to lunch with the Prime Minister for?" MacGregor said—and he was very shirty about this and so was Geoff Stewart—"Don't bloody well ask us, we weren't invited." So off I went to lunch with the Prime Minister, but I couldn't understand it. When I got there, being a lowly sapper and all, I just stood over in the corner and had a few beers and wondered "Why am I here?" I was just about to sneak out through the back door when a young artillery captain came over and asked me if I was Snowy Wilson. I said yes, and he said, "Come over here, the Prime Minister wants to talk to you."

'It was Harold Holt. "Ah, you're Snowy Wilson, are you?" he asks. "Where's your twin brother?" I said, "Up on the front beach digging a bloody well, where I should be, and should have been for about the last four hours." "Well, why isn't he here?" he says, and the Prime Minister rips into this young captain and asks him why my twin brother wasn't there too. "Well, I rung the troop and they said there was only one Wilson in it," says the captain. I just burst out laughing. I said, "My twin brother's surname is Coolburra—he's a full-blooded Aboriginal."

'What had happened was my mother had been very cheesed off at the reception that Harold Holt got in Perth when he visited there in 1966. She and my father decided they'd send him a bit of a cheer-up telegram wishing him all the best for his tour to South Vietnam and saying, if there's any possibility whilst you're there, please say hello to our son Snow and his twin brother Bill. And nobody ever put two and two together. The people in Saigon that were organising all the tours just looked at the list and said there's only one Wilson there, we'll just send him. When I found out I bloody near wet myself laughing.'

■ ■ ■ ■

Dave Cook was another who found the comradeship of fighting a common foe outweighed the racism that was (and still is) prevalent in Australia.

'I have been aware of racialism in Australia since I was eight years old,' says Dave. 'But I never ran across any in the Australian Army. In the American Army, yes, because they used to live in different lines and yet go out and fight together. I just couldn't understand that.'

Dave was one of the wilder elements in the troop—but he was also one of the best forward scouts in the Australian Army. One of the reasons you could trust Dave to lead you through jungle without getting himself or anyone else killed was that he respected the Vietcong's fighting ability. 'He was a very cunning enemy,' recalls Dave. 'That's why whenever I got one of them in my sights I never let them get out.'

Dave was also partly responsible for a frosty exchange of letters between Sandy MacGregor and General Williamson, commander of the 173rd Airborne Brigade. Three Field Troop had adopted the Cherry Bar in Bien Hoa and they were such good customers that they were allowed to sign chits for their drinks and pay up at the end of the month. But one afternoon when there were about eight of them there, a bunch of Americans had invaded the place and were causing such a commotion that the manager called the Shore Patrol. Eventually the MPs bowled up and threw all the Yanks out, then told the Aussies to get out too. They were outraged, saying that they hadn't been causing any problems, the manager hadn't told them to go and, anyway, the American MPs had no jurisdiction over them. They made it clear they weren't leaving.

'We got precious little time off in those days as it was, so there was no way we were going back to camp,' says Dave. 'That's when a bit of an altercation broke out.'

The MP's sergeant went outside and a few minutes later returned with their lieutenant, a tall black guy who was armed with a huge 'night stick' style police baton. He withdrew the baton from his belt and rested it on his shoulder. Dave Cook, who was about half his size, fronted up to him.

'What are you going to do with that, you black bastard?' Dave asked, and the MP officer raised the baton as if he was going to bash him. Big mistake. Dave thumped him in the chest and suddenly it was all on. Fists and feet flew in the tiny bar and tables were wrecked and windows smashed as the melee spilled out into the street. Mick Lee and Keith Kermode managed to overturn one of the MPs' jeeps (to the cheers of other Americans looking on) before they were finally subdued with the help of reinforcements.

Next thing, the eight Aussies were being marched to the MPs' headquarters. They must have made a strange procession—a jeep in front and another at the rear, with the troop members in the middle and flanked on either side by a row of MPs. And every couple of minutes the procession would stop when one of the men tried to escape down an alley, only to be caught and dragged back into line. Eventually they got all of them to the MPs' HQ, where they were confronted by a desk sergeant who would brook no nonsense from them, despite their protests that their handcuffs were too tight.

Then up piped 'Barney' Barnett in a posh voice none of his mates had ever heard before, demanding a glass of water and complaining that he'd never been subjected to such treatment in his life before, being a 'sapper'. The Yanks all looked at each other. What the hell was a sapper? Barney showed them his ID card. 'SPR Barnett', it said. 'Special Privileged Rank,' he explained. That seemed to impress the Yanks, and they let Barney go.

'So we all started yelling that we were sappers too,' says Dennis Ayoub. 'But they wouldn't listen. Eventually everybody quietened down—except Dave and I. So they let all the others go but insisted they were taking the two of us back to camp to have us put on a charge. Dave was not best pleased at this, so while we were driving along in the MPs' jeep, he started dismantling their radio and throwing the parts out onto the road.

'That did it with the MPs. They jumped on us and handcuffed us to the frame of the jeep, standing up and spread-eagled in the back. First they drove us to 1 RAR, but they didn't want us. Then they took us to 3 Field Troop. But those handcuffs bloody hurt. One of them had stood on Dave's cuffs so as to close them as tight as they could.'

For Dave, that was worse than a dozen detentions or punishment details. 'They had the handcuffs on us so tight that they damaged the nerves in our hands,' he says.

Sandy MacGregor saw red. These were highly skilled engineers whose manual dexterity could mean the difference between life and death. Now they were being half-crippled by their own side. So he wrote to General Williamson and told him in no uncertain terms that he'd appreciate it if his MPs would be a little less brutal when they found it necessary to arrest his men. The general replied that he'd appreciate it if Sandy's men would be a little less brutal when they were being arrested by his MPs.

Dave later became a legend within the engineers when he shot himself in the foot only a week before he was due to fly home. Stories about that incident abound. Some said it was deliberate, which is stupid because it only meant he ended up in hospital and got back to Australia *after* everybody else. Some say Dave was practising his quick draw with a Colt revolver he had acquired. Dave did fancy himself as a gunfighter, but he never shot himself when he was playing John Wayne. Another story that did the rounds was that Dave was shot by a sniper who got him in the toe. Keith Kermode got into a fight with another sapper on his second tour, when he insisted that that story was bullshit.

The simple truth was that Dave was lying in his bunk cleaning his army-issue pistol when it went off. 'Dave was such a good soldier and such a wild young man that he was always a bigger danger to himself than the Vietcong were to him,' says Sandy. 'Even in the middle of a war, he was his own worst enemy.'

The third black member of 3 Field Troop was Bill Unmeopa, a Thursday Islander, who was also a very good soldier. Bill was a bit more mature and more responsible than the others, but he refused to take a higher rank until he returned to Vietnam later on, probably because he felt uncomfortable with the idea of issuing orders to men who had been his mates. He may also have been uneasy with the idea of being in command of white guys. In any case, he got over it, and both he and Dave Cook served with distinction as corporals in their second tours of Vietnam.

# 6. RAIN IN THE RICE BOWL

Three Field Troop had barely spent a week and a half back in camp after Operation Hump when they were away again on New Life, which was the troop's biggest single operation, both in terms of the numbers of men deployed—46 sappers—and the length of time they were away from camp.

New Life took them about 100 kilometres east-north-east of Saigon to an area of low land near the village of Vo Dat. The region contained one of Vietnam's 'rice bowls' and the troop's main job was to rebuild a road through swampy areas and repair bridges so that the 10th Infantry Division ARVN could move into and through the area quickly. There's nothing the Vietcong liked better than seeing a few thousand American and South Vietnamese troops strung out along

10 miles of a jungle road, waiting for the blokes at the front to find some way of crossing a river.

The infantry were going up to Vo Dat to protect the rice crop, firstly so that the South Vietnamese could harvest it in relative peace; secondly, so that the Vietcong didn't get their hands on it. Sandy MacGregor's notes described the land: 'The area, as one can imagine it, is flat and low-lying. Many parts of the country are swamp. Flanking the bowl were extensive mountain ranges with their accompanying heavy forest cover. Many streams laced the area—they were wide with the usual eroded bank typical of lowland waterways. Secondary growth existed in part around the higher area but there was little vegetation with the exception of long [1 metre high] grass.'

The operation was conducted by 173rd Airborne Brigade, plus two attached infantry battalions. Basically, they were up against two deadlines: they had to get the road fixed up so that the 10th Division ARVN could use it, and they had to get through in time to save the rice. So they worked flat-out, building and repairing roads and small bridges while still dealing with the odd tunnel and booby trap.

Often they were upgrading what was little more than a mud track to the point where it could sustain a pounding from all the heavy trucks and other vehicles it was due to carry, or repairing it after they'd rumbled through. At one point the road had been carved up so badly that all 3 Field Troop's vehicles had to be towed through with the help of armoured personnel carriers. Road building is a big job at the best of times but stuck in the middle of a Vietnamese swamp, it meant cutting down trees for timber, opening up gravel pits where none had existed before and carting the materials before the work could even begin. And it rained . . . a lot.

One night the rain was lashing down and the engineers were up to their armpits in bog and mud. The machines were slipping all over the place but they were getting the job done and making good headway until they reached a gully which, since it was getting dark, Sandy MacGregor decided they'd bridge the next day. No sooner had they got to the edge of the gully than an infantry company from 1 RAR appeared at the other side. The infantry were supposed to be there to guard the engineers and, if anything, they were wetter and more miserable than the engineers were. Their Aussie commander was in a mood as foul as the weather. Between the two groups, the road had been blown in seven places and water was raging in torrents through the gaps.

The major ordered Sandy and his men to cross the divide and meet up with them. Sandy refused, saying he'd have to bulldoze his way across, tow the vehicles through one by one, and then the next day have to bridge the gap which would by then be more than 100 metres wide. It would be a waste of time, energy and materials and would hold up the construction of a proper crossing which he needed to complete by the next night.

There isn't an army in the world where refusing to obey an order doesn't come with serious consequences but that's exactly what Sandy did. He then took the precaution of contacting battalion HQ, the major's boss, and telling them of his predicament. The order for the troop to stay where they were and for the infantry company to withdraw came loud and clear and Sandy breathed a huge sigh of relief. The Aussies who had slogged their way through rain-soaked jungle turned and disappeared back to where they'd come from. To Sandy, it was just a victory for common sense. To the infantry company, it would have been nothing more or less than bloody engineers acting up again.

The next day the raging waters subsided and the troop built a causeway with anything that was around—wood, charcoal and gravel—then had a light aluminium bridge choppered in to put over the main 6-metre gap.

Later, on an air reconnaissance, Sandy spotted a large 35-metre steel bridge which had been sabotaged and was broken in the middle with the approach ramps at both ends missing. This bridge had to be repaired before the 10th Division could get through. It was sitting up several feet above the roadway, stranded in mid-air on the concrete pillars at both ends. Its back was broken about a quarter of the way along. Sandy had an idea which seemed outrageously ambitious at first. What they'd do was 'cut' the bridge with explosives at the point at which it was broken and at the pillars at the other end. Thus released, the bridge would drop onto the river bank and all they'd have to do would be to fill the trenches at either end and they'd have a working crossing again.

The American engineers thought the Aussies were mad, but to build a new bridge would have meant removing the old one, putting up the new structure—which would have been 35 metres long—then carting in 20 truckloads of gravel from 10 kilometres away for the approaches. The Americans bet a case of beer that the plan to drop the bridge wouldn't work, but the stakes were higher than that: 3 Field Troop's and the whole engineering corps' reputations seemed to rest on this trick.

Using both electrical and detonation cord so that the charges would go off at exactly the same time and the bridge wouldn't be twisted by the blasts, there was nothing to do but hope for the best and press the button. They won the case of beer but if they had failed, the whole division would have been strung out along the road for another day.

Once the road had been seen to and the 10th Division had come and gone, things quietened down for the troop. The operation had already been a great success. They had opened up the road, built at least four bridges and several little crossings and saved a whole day, which is very significant in an operation. A division strung out along a road is not a pretty sight—especially after the enemy gets it in their sights.

■ ■ ■ ■

Both Sandy and Lieutenant Geoff Stewart, his number two, were on Operation New Life (with 46 sappers), which was unusual. Geoff was normally left to keep things ticking over in camp while Sandy went into the field with the men. But they needed every man they could get. As well as all the roadworks, they were extending the landing zones, conducting tunnel and village searches and even filling in ditches, which pleased the local villagers. Part of the plan was to undertake 'civic action' work, to make life easier for the villagers in the area and convince them that the Aussies were the good guys in this war. A lot of the time this simply involved putting a grader over their roads or levelling their village squares, but on at least one occasion they put up a bridge which was purely for local rather than strategic use.

Nine days into the operation they were given responsibility for the road between Vo Xu and Mapu—about 15 kilometres of the soggiest marsh possible. They found a destroyed bridge about 6 metres long over a creek in the middle of Mapu village. On the other side of it Geoff Stewart spotted a blue vehicle, which looked like a panel van. Mapu was a Vietcong-dominated village and, now that the Allies were in the area in force, the local villagers abandoned the place in droves and left for safer areas. They probably left while the Vietcong were still in control as they wouldn't have wanted to be caught up in any fighting that followed.

The troop put a new bridge in and were told that the

blue vehicle—a Willys jeep—was abandoned by the local Vietcong boss, who by now had become 'just another villager'. The spoils of war were there for the taking. The troop needed another vehicle and they weren't likely to get one through the army system. First they checked it for booby traps, then Rod Goater, the RAEME mechanic, took a look at it to see if he thought he could get it to work. Rod reckoned he could fix it, but only back in base camp at Bien Hoa. So Sandy proposed towing the thing back to Bien Hoa with the troop's Land Rover and returning on a C-130 transport plane. He couldn't do it on his own so he asked Mick Lee and Peter Ash—two of the tougher nuts in the troop—if they wanted to go too, with Rod there to look after the mechanical side of business. The three of them needed no second invitation.

'I jumped at the chance because I was just sitting around on my gun all day watching old blokes walking around a peanut farm,' recalls Mick Lee. 'It was just to break the monotony. I said, "You beaut!" And I thought at the time, "Well, not bad—all the guys he could have picked and he's picked me."'

So off they set, towing their spoils of war and feeling a bit like schoolboys who'd skipped classes to have a jaunt in the countryside. Everything was going fine until they hit a village about halfway home. It was hidden round a corner and they were in the village before they knew it—and right in the middle of an ambush.

'The first thing I noticed was that there were bodies strewn all over the road but it was only seconds later when the first shots rang out,' says Sandy. 'Mick and I immediately headed for the ditch in the Land Rover and, of course, Peter and Rod [who were being towed] had no option but to follow. Obviously, we'd just driven straight into the middle of an ambush, minutes after it had happened. But the curious thing was that the dead bodies looked like Vietcong, which meant that the people who were shooting at us were on our side.'

Sandy tried shouting at them in English, but just got shot at, so then he tried French, since he reckoned they must be ARVN and their officer, at least, would know the language of their former colonial masters. The blokes made their contribution too.

'We shouted in every bloody language we could think of,' says Rod. 'Some of it wasn't very polite.'

Eventually the shooting died down, but the foursome had no idea whether it was safer to go on, to turn back or just sit still. Their problem was that they were in an Australian Land Rover towing a Vietcong Willys jeep. The South Vietnamese soldiers, who can't have been very familiar with Australian equipment and markings, would realise neither of the vehicles were theirs or American. In fact, they probably only recognised the Willys as a Vietcong vehicle and assumed it was an enemy patrol.

There was a spotter plane flying over every so often so the Aussie foursome made huge letters U and S out of stones—it was easier than trying to spell out 'Aussie'—and after a while the plane came back and dropped a canister on a mini-parachute. In it there was a message to proceed with caution and 'avoid contact'.

The foursome would have been only too happy to follow the latter instruction, although they didn't see how they could avoid contact if the contact didn't want to avoid them. Sandy asked the men if they wanted to cut and run and dump the Willys or go on. But they were all for going on back to camp and taking the Willys with them, if that was at all possible. It was obvious that the ARVN wanted them to get the hell out of their way, so they took off and left them to it. On the way back they had to clear two Vietcong road blocks and passed a huge convoy of US and ARVN troops heading in the opposite direction. But they got the Willys home and jumped the transport plane back to Vo Dat before anyone missed them.

The Willys was put back into working order fairly quickly once they got back to Bien Hoa and it became something of a mascot for the troop who christened it 'Ucdaloi'—after the Vietnamese word for Australian. Even today, the sappers remember what a boost to morale it was to have their own little runabout. They found it, they brought it home, they spent their casino profits on it and they fixed it up. It was such a typically engineer thing to do that they almost forgot that it nearly cost four of them their lives.

After they'd taken the Willys back to camp and returned to the operation, life became very, very boring. Even the infantry were a little bit bored. They were going on patrols but not much was happening. For the last week of Operation New Life they went about 30 kilometres south to conduct straightforward search-and-destroy missions near some abandoned villages, and came across some new booby traps.

Booby traps fell into three categories: the crude, the commonplace and the fiendishly bloody clever. The crude were usually variations on your basic bear-trap—a covered hole in the ground concealing bamboo or steel spikes. The commonplace were landmines which blew up when you stood on or drove over them or DH-10 mines (like Australian Claymores) which would be hidden in bushes and would explode sideways into whoever was passing. The clever ones were mostly bombs of some kind or another, with ingenious methods used to conceal and detonate them. Some of them weren't even bombs. One of the simplest was a bullet pointing upwards in a small hole in the ground, with a nail underneath it to act as a firing pin. All you had to do was to step on it and you'd literally shoot yourself in the foot.

The Vietcong were great at adapting what they could get

their hands on to put to deadly use. Often grenades were used in conjunction with trip-wires or artillery shells, which would be electrically detonated by an observer hiding somewhere nearby. And while some of the grenades were the standard-issue military type, there were a lot of homemade bombs, such as shrapnel packed around explosives inside a tin can.

Trip-wires were popular, but there were other, less obvious ways of setting them up. Grenades would be attached to a line strung high over a road to get anyone who was travelling on top of a vehicle. A bomb would be planted under a flagpole and attached to the cord from which a North Vietnamese flag was flying—pity the poor sod who couldn't resist pulling the flag down. Bombs and shells would be hung over roads either to be detonated over Allied forces, or even just as an early warning of their approach. Tunnels, caves and huts could be booby-trapped, as could rice bags, souvenir items in abandoned camps, approach roads and entrance ways to rice or equipment caches. One favourite trick was to put a fairly obvious trip-wire across a path, but have another, better-hidden wire a couple of metres farther on that would catch anyone who was lulled into a false sense of security.

The two-stage door trap we described earlier. Another fiendish trap was the 'takeaway'—imagine five metal spikes in the shape of five dots on a domino with the four outer ones sloped into the middle and all of them with fish-hook style barbs at their points. The idea was that it would be buried in a hole in the ground and when you stepped on it, the central spike went through your foot and the four corner spikes dug into your leg. It was called the takeaway because you would not be going anywhere without it still attached to you.

All these devices—the bombs themselves and the way they were set up—were the engineers' responsibility. Most of them were completely new to the Australians so, right from the start, Sandy established what became known as the Bomb Museum. Whenever the engineers found a new kind of bomb, they'd take it back to camp for closer inspection.

'One very good thing that Sandy instigated—and I was delighted that he did—was "the Museum", as we called it,' says Warren Lennon, Officer Commanding 1 Field Squadron Royal Australian Engineers, who took command when the main body of soldiers arrived from Australia. 'It was a collection of bombs, grenades and booby traps that they brought back from operations. Part of his procedure, and one that we adopted, was whenever we found a new type of booby trap or device, we deloused it, took it back, and everyone would be instructed on how it was put together and how you defused it.

'Indeed, before every operation, every member of every mini-team went over to the museum and they handled every bit of ordnance that we had there just to refresh their memory that this was how this thing worked and this is how to fix it. I think that was a useful piece of training and a useful reinforcement of the need to really know your job. Sandy started that and I was delighted that he shared it with the rest of us when we arrived. We introduced that as standard operating procedure.'

Then, so that everyone could become familiar with the bombs, they sent detailed notes back to the School of Military Engineering in Australia so that the sappers being trained there would have a better idea of what to expect when they got to Vietnam. It was certainly appreciated by the troops who came after them.

Sometimes, however, their best efforts were to no avail. For instance, there were two types of Vietcong stick grenade. One had a time fuse, so that you could pull the pin and still have time to throw it. The other was instantaneous and was obviously designed either to be thrown with a long line attached to it or to be used specifically for booby traps. The trouble was that there was no way you could tell them apart and the engineers never found out how to do so, in all the time they were there. One infantry corporal was killed when he tried to pull the pin and throw one that had an instantaneous fuse. It exploded before it had even left his hand.

One day, in frustration, Sandy decided to cut one open to find out what was inside. He was in the area they used for defusing bombs, sawing away with a hacksaw, when the whole stick grenade fell apart in his hands. You have never seen anyone move so fast, he recalls. It obviously wasn't on an instantaneous fuse or he wouldn't have had time to pick up the whole assembly and throw it as far as he could into the nearby scrub, shouting for everyone within earshot to get down. Nothing happened. And it was a very sheepish young captain who emerged from the bomb disposal area, still none the wiser about how to tell the different types of grenade apart. But at least he now knew it was possible to throw, duck and shout all at the same time.

# 7. SEX AND THE SINGLE SOLDIER

As you'd expect with a bunch of 60-odd lads, some of whom were very odd indeed and most of whom were barely out of their teens, sex inevitably reared its ugly head. That's not to say that sex is necessarily ugly. But it's reasonable to assume that the attitudes of callow youths, for whom the distinctions between the roles of liberators and conquerors had become fudged, were far from pretty. These were raw young men who, had they been at home, would have been enjoying the dubious benefits of the era of so-called free love of the sixties. Back then, Australian men were not renowned as the most enlightened when it came to women and neither were many celebrated for their tolerance of other races. So we can safely say that in the mid-sixties the majority of Vietnam pioneers would not have lost too much sleep fretting over the ethics of why so many young Vietnamese women were so freely available.

Make that 'readily' available, for in Vietnam, they discovered, love was definitely not free—but it was available at a price. And the currency wasn't always dollars and cents. Dennis Ayoub recalled one of the perks of being on home duties. The third of the troop that wasn't out on patrol or on guard detail had to help look after the domestic side of matters. And part of that meant cleaning up in the kitchen and disposing of the garbage.

'The Yanks sent round a truck twice a week to pick up our food scraps,' Dennis said. 'But when it was hot weather, our scraps stank so much that we got the OK to do our own drops on the days in between. The tip was just outside the perimeter fence, about a kilometre away. The first couple of blokes to do the run were surprised to find these old Vietnamese women scavenging on the tip looking for anything they could make use of and for any food that was still edible. Pretty soon the blokes got the message that the old dears would give them a blow job or a hand job if they let them have first look through the bins before they dumped them. But these women were really old . . .'

Then Keith Kermode discovered a Vietnamese village by following some kids he saw clambering through the wire fence. 'It never occurred to me that the fence was there to keep them out, or even to keep us in,' says Keith. 'I just saw the kids going through the gap in the fence and followed them. It's like they say about crawling over broken glass . . .'

The lads may have been sex mad, but they weren't stupid. With typical engineers' cunning, they reckoned that if they upped the ante, they'd get a better class of service.

'We got two clean steel garbage bins with handles and kept them scrubbed up well so that they always looked new,' said Dennis. 'Then we made sure only the best food scraps went into it: half loaves of bread, bits of meat, ends of roasts, tins. We didn't put any shit in it—no tea bags or custard or gravy—all that went in the other bins. When it was nearly full, the driver and his mate—you always had to have someone riding shotgun when you went outside the gate—dumped the other stuff at the tip then headed back down the road towards the village.'

The place he was talking about wasn't even a collection of bamboo huts—it was little more than a clearing in the scrub. The houses were mostly chicken coops which had been commandeered either because of overcrowding or because the main building had been destroyed. These people were the poorest of the poor Vietnamese peasantry. To them it mattered little whose army was occupying their country. Their main priority was survival. It was, however, out of bounds. There could have been any number of Vietcong hiding in or near it. But a young soldier's hormones will lead him into dangers his officers would never order him to face.

'The idea was to drive up to the village and park the truck in a place where you had a clear view of the village and the road out,' said Dennis. 'The driver had the first privilege, while the shotgun hopped into the driver's seat and kept the engine running. Our main fears were, in this order, Vietcong, Military Police, detection by Aussie gunners or infantry, since the area was forward of their wire, and of course, MacGregor. The modus operandi had been set up by the previous guys and the rate of exchange was one bin, one root. After a couple of weeks, when we went down there they had the girls lined up waiting. We were bloody mad. The village was off limits and it could have been riddled with Vietcong.'

Fortunately for them they were never caught, either by the Vietcong or Sandy MacGregor, even if he occasionally wondered why the polished up, well-fed garbage can had been immortalised as 'the Root Bin'. But the fun didn't end there, according to Dennis. 'Afterwards we'd let all the kids climb on the back of the truck then, when we were driving along the road we'd start the tipper and they'd be screaming and sliding off the back and trying to see who could hang on the longest. They'd be covered in shit and slipping everywhere. It's a wonder we didn't kill one of the poor little bastards. But they loved it!'

Although not all the drivers took advantage of the sexual

perk, there was a lot of competition among the other men to ride shotgun on the trips to the dump. And being put on home duties as punishment didn't carry quite the same sting as peeling potatoes.

'What you have to understand is that a leave pass to Saigon was an arduous duty,' explained Dennis. 'See, you had to get up at five in the morning, then be at battalion at seven, all scrubbed up, to get your name ticked off. Then you'd get on a truck to go into town. When you got there you had to get drunk, fed and laid as many times as you could manage—or afford—then get back on the truck at three o'clock. Now that's a pretty tough task, especially when you've got a thirst as long as from here to Bourke.' So the men had their fun where they could find it, and often weren't too particular about who had been there before them. Inevitably, sexually transmitted diseases were prevalent and although they didn't have the deadly connotations they bear in these days of AIDS, they did have embarrassing side effects.

Since STDs were considered 'self-inflicted wounds', they had to be reported to the commanding officer. Sparrow Christie recalls having to front up to the doctor's assistant with a dose of gonorrhoea. 'The worst part was that I had to stand in his office and drop my daks, so's he could have a look.' Mick McGrath, on the other hand, seemed to be impervious to venereal disease. And another sapper, whom he has declined to name, was always demanding to know his 'secret'. The truth was that Mick didn't have a secret, but one night, when he found himself out on the town with this particular mate, there was no escape. 'We went into the brothel and he's going on and on at me to tell him,' says Mick. 'So I said that what he should do is have a piss and wash his dick straight after he'd done it. We get settled down with these sheilas and everything's going fine and the next thing I know there's all this shouting and his bird's screaming blue murder and calling for the cops. So I rush round and the stupid bastard only shagged her, pulled it out and then pissed all over the place while trying to aim for the tin in the corner of the room. That was the last time I gave anybody advice.'

The bars in Bien Hoa were little more than brothels. Australian soldiers differed from their American counterparts in many respects, including how they behaved with the bar girls. While the US troops would be happy to spend all evening being entertained by the girls before taking them upstairs, the Aussies liked to spend the evening drinking with their mates before hooking up with the girls. It was just like the dances at home: blokes at one end of the bar, women at the other.

Another reason was the bar girls would only stay with the guys if they bought them Saigon Tea, a ridiculously expensive drink which was little more than coloured water. The profits of this little scam, of course, went to the bar owner. Later the girls would take the men upstairs to what was essentially a dormitory with the beds separated by sheets hung from wires. If the men refused to buy them their drinks, which they often did, the girls would call them 'Cheap Charlies' and go off in search of more sociable customers.

'Work hard—play hard', their unofficial motto, was exercised to the full. The truckies like Keith Kermode and Mick McGrath used to smuggle men out so they could go to nearby brothels when they were supposed to be in camp.

'Keith and I, we used to quite often take the blokes out through the gate in the back of the tippers,' says Mick. 'They used to lie down on the back of the tipper and I had a particular brothel I used to take them to. The mama-san there used to know me and every time I took in half a dozen blokes I used to get a girl for free.'

All of this illicit sexual activity went on despite rumours of a new and deadly form of sexually transmitted disease that had allegedly appeared among the troops.

'It was called Vietnam Rose,' says Keith. 'It was a rumour that there was a form of VD so bad that you had to go home. It was bullshit that was put out by the bloody padre. I think he must have started that one . . . or the RAP. I heard many times, if you got it you might as well put a gun to your head.'

Mick Lee had heard the rumours too: 'That was the incurable jack, they reckoned. The old story went if you had it you were put forward scout 'cause no one had a better chance of being hit than your forward scout, of course.'

An interesting postscript to these tales comes from Mick McGrath, who, for several months, had a steady Vietnamese girlfriend in Vung Tau (which probably explains his avoidance of STDs). Sandy MacGregor was pretty strict on discipline but it's in the engineer's nature to find a way over, round or under whatever obstacles get in his way. That is, after all, what he does for a living. How 3 Field Troop got round the military discipline system is perfectly illustrated by the story of Mick's run-in with the Military Police or Provos.

'I had parked my truck outside the girlfriend's house and these Provos come marching in. "Right," they say, "you're nicked!" "What for?" I ask. "Abandoning a military vehicle." "I didn't abandon it . . . I've got the keys here." "And leaving your weapons unattended . . ." "I've got my rifle with me . . ." I wasn't stupid. I always took my rifle. "What about the six hand grenades rolling about on the cab floor?" says one of them. "What the fuck are they for?" "It's dangerous out there," I say, getting a bit cheeky. "Don't you know there's a war on?"

'That pisses them right off and they're booking me for this charge and that charge and then one of them says "I've got my eye on you, McGrath. You won't be able to breathe in this town without me sticking you on for it." Sure enough, every time I went out, this bastard would turn up and hassle me for no reason, and always try to provoke me. One night a gang of us were out on the town and I saw him on his own in a bar. I went up to him and said "You've got it in for me, haven't you?" And to cut a long story short, we dragged him outside and I got a couple of the bigger lads to hold him. He thought I was going to bash him up.

'But I'm not that stupid. If I'd done that I'd have ended up in jail, no worries. So while they held him, I pissed all over his boots. "Now," I says, "Go back and tell everybody what I did to you." To tell you the truth, I was worried after that. And a couple of days later I went to Corporal John Opie who handled MacGregor's mail and all that, to find out what charges I was on and when they'd be coming up. You see, all matters of discipline like that would be referred to MacGregor as a matter of course. And I hadn't yet been pulled up for even one of the things that Provo bastard had nicked me for. I was worried that it was all building up and I was going to cop it all at once.

'Anyway, I ask what the score is and John just laughs. "Mick," he says, "I just read them to see what everybody's been up to then throw them in the bin. MacGregor never gets to see most of them. And, believe me, you're not the worst. Not by a long shot."'

John Opie rightly reckoned that even a wayward engineer

was worth more to the army in the field than counting the hours in a punishment block. And that is very much an engineer's solution to a common problem. Discipline and morale both, to a great extent, remained intact. Or, to put it another way, what the eye doesn't see the heart doesn't grieve.

# 8. KNIGHTS IN SINKING ARMOUR

The week before Christmas 1965, half the troop went on an operation called Smash, which was supposed to be a straight-forward search-and-destroy mission. As it turned out they spent most of their time searching for each other. Smash was set up to be a simple four-day sweep through an area to the east of Saigon about halfway between Bien Hoa and Vung Tau. The troop, as part of 1 RAR, were to move south while 173rd Airborne moved north to meet them.

It should have been a stroll, and would have been, had they not been totally unused to that kind of jungle and laden down with all their engineering gear. On that operation, the 3 Field Troop men were divided up into seven combat teams of four engineers, plus a headquarters element, all attached to battalion HQ. They were there to deal with tunnels, booby traps, bridges—all the usual stuff. But in truth it was little more than an infantry exercise, and one which they would have been perfectly capable of handling if they'd been carrying the same loads as the infantrymen.

To give you an idea, your basic infantryman on a three-day operation would carry three days' food, first line ammunition—for his machine gun or his rifle—his first aid kit, a change of gear, his hutchie, a kind of one-man tent, and all that sort of stuff. He'd have his weapon too, of course, and as much water as he could get, say three water bottles because they were getting supplies only once a day. In fact, there were some days when they got no supplies because they were employing jungle tactics, which means you don't have helicopters flying in to resupply you all the time. And of course they'd have all their chlorine and water purification tablets so that if they found some water they could fill up and make it drinkable. All in all, that would have come to 25, maybe 30 kilos.

But that was only for the ordinary foot soldiers. Sappers had to carry extra things like explosives, detonators and detonator cord, pliers, torches, extra communication cable, telephone cable and tear gas grenades, smoke grenades, picks and shovels. There would have been five or more kilos of extra weight for each man. You're talking about 18- to 19-year-old guys, some of whom weighed little more than

55 kilos, carrying 35 to 40 kilo packs. It soon showed. The first night the engineers were plodding along some way behind the rest of the battalion and Sandy MacGregor started to get the uneasy feeling that they weren't going to make it to camp before dark. When he finally overcame his embarrassment and radioed to the infantrymen ahead of them that they were in danger of getting lost, the infantry sent back a scout who led them forward to their camp site at the rear of the main battalion.

As usual, they set about their normal tasks: digging weapons pits, putting up the hutchies, manning the guard posts, and cutting vines and creepers to use as a simple but effective perimeter fence—to stop the men accidentally wandering out rather than to prevent the enemy from coming in. The trouble was, it was so dark they literally couldn't see their hands in front of their faces. People who have lived all their lives in the city have probably never seen true darkness. Even in the country a pitch black night is rare. This was the kind of darkness you'd expect at the bottom of a coal mine—the face of a luminous watch 10 metres away shone like a lighthouse on a moonless night.

The result was that they barely managed their basic security measures. When they changed the guard, a couple of guys wandered out past the perimeter and almost got lost. It was chaos. The next couple of days they made sure they kept up with the infantry boys and the decision to establish the night defensive harbour was taken a bit sooner than on the first evening. And when they made camp, you've never seen weapons pits dug or perimeter vines cut faster in your life. Every hutchie had strings or wires running from it to its weapons pit and the latrines so the men could find their way back in the night.

'I wasn't taking any chances that I'd have to tell anybody that I'd lost any men—not when "lost" actually meant lost,' recalls Sandy.

Apart from the troop's problems with the dark, Smash was a non-event but the troop realised for the first time that they would be operating as a self-contained infantry unit—that is, they were expected to defend themselves rather than having infantry protecting them. With that in mind, Sandy pointed out that they had no machine guns, and they were immediately issued with two M-60s, which was a great relief . . . until they realised that nobody actually knew how to fire them.

On 1 January 1966, Sandy and 36 men were flown out to an area near the Cambodian border called the Plain of Reeds, ostensibly to complete one seven-day operation. By the time they returned to camp two weeks later, with a second, unexpected operation under their belts, they'd have lost a mate and the whole thinking about the way the Vietcong were conducting their side of the war would be changed radically.

But first they had to deal with Operation Marauder. The area they were working in was riddled with canals and swamps and six out of seven APCs (armoured personnel carriers) were bogged to the gunwales. Normally they can move through that sort of stuff but if they stop, they sink. As they travelled through this swampy area they came to irrigation ditches which were just like tank ditches—vertical sides, 2 metres deep and about 4 metres wide. If an APC got in that it would never have got out in a million years, so they stopped and propped . . . and sank. It has to be said that the armoured boys are pretty proud—as, after Long Tan, they are entitled to be—and these APCs can usually swim across water, so they were in no hurry to say 'come and help us'. It's usually the other way round and infantry are looking for their help.

Anyway, by the time 3 Field Troop got to them there was only one APC that wasn't bogged. Sandy wanted to lay a track for that APC so that it could go along until it was within rope reach of the APCs that were bogged, then pull it out. Corporal 'Froggy' Seddon suggested using the steel wire ropes off their own dozers and they radioed back to brigade HQ and asked them to send out some timber and pierced steel plate so that they could lay tracks to the bogged APCs. But when the Chinook helicopter arrived, the pilot said he'd cancelled the order off his own bat because he reckoned he could pull the APCs out himself.

The Chinook is a big, powerful machine and is often used

to carry field guns and fairly heavy loads, but an APC? In any case, lifting wasn't the plan. They attached the steel cable to the Chinook's hook (under the aircraft) and the first APC. Then the chopper pulled the APC along as much as up—or at least it tried to. It was incredible to see this huge machine only a couple of metres off the ground, straining at an angle of 45 degrees to pull the APC out. Captain Rothwell, who was the infantry commander of the company at that stage, said, 'You know, if the rope broke the Chinook would just spin head over tail until it hit the ground.' Eventually the APC moved and a big cheer went up from all the lads. But when they tried to get the next one out, the Chinook strained and strained but just couldn't budge it. The helicopter pilot who cancelled that supplies order suddenly didn't look like so much of a hero. Eventually, when they got the stuff they needed, the troop built their roadway to the next APC and attached the cable to the two APCs that were now free. That one moved and now they had three free vehicles. The next thing to do was attach those three to the fourth and so on.

It took a couple of days and a hell of a lot of effort plus a very uncomfortable night spent in the swamp before they freed the last APC. But it was just the morale booster the troop needed for what lay immediately ahead. The fact that they weren't going straight back to Bien Hoa, as expected, when the choppers started arriving on the Plain of Reeds was as much a surprise to Sandy MacGregor as it was to anyone else. The troop rendezvoused at the landing zone ready for 'sticks' of helicopters to take them off. A stick of choppers could be, say, seven helicopters. They'd land and six blokes would run forward to board each chopper and then they'd all take off together. Each stick would have two helicopter gunships guarding it. Just before they took off, the order came through that they were going into the Ho Bo Woods area north of Saigon.

Three Field Troop was supposed to be part of a blocking force, going into an area that hadn't been entered much before and which was believed to be an enemy stronghold. The reason for the sudden change of plan was almost certainly to outsmart the spies at the ARVN headquarters in Saigon. Most of the guys didn't know about the change of plan until they got on the chopper.

'That pissed me off, I tell you,' says Les Colmer. 'Every time you go on operation you all look forward to that last day, that last hour and getting on that chopper and going home, going back to camp. Only this time we got in the bloody chopper and MacGregor told us we weren't going back to camp. I couldn't believe it. I asked him what he was talking about. And he told me they'd switched us in mid-stride and we had another op to do on the way back.'

It seemed like a dirty trick at the time but it probably saved hundreds of Australian lives.

# 9. ONWARD AND DOWNWARD

Operation Crimp was a turning point for 3 Field Troop. It had a tragic outcome that bonded the men together as never before and made them the soldiers they needed to be. In a larger historical perspective, it could also have been a turning point in the whole Vietnam War, as journalist Chris Masters said in his TV documentary *Page One*. They were, literally, right on top of the Vietcong's southern HQ.

When 3 Field Troop joined the infantry sweep of the area, they expected there would be some tunnels but had no idea that there would be virtually an underground city, let alone suspect what it contained. It would turn out to be the headquarters of the Vietcong of the Cho Lon/Gia Dinh area of Saigon, the nerve centre from which the enemy ran their forward operations in the country's south-east and later masterminded their final assault on Saigon. But as far as the troop was concerned, it was just another operation tagged on to the one they'd just finished. Another job when they should have been heading back to base.

The Ho Bo woods are about 4 kilometres to the west of the 'Iron Triangle', an area north-east of Saigon which was known to have an unusually high concentration of Vietcong troops. The Iron Triangle hadn't been entered in any great strength for about three years and there was a strong feeling among the top brass that the Vietcong had not only re-infiltrated the area after it had been heavily shelled and bombed, but had established the southern command HQ there. They were right, but what they didn't know was that finding and destroying the Vietcong base was a lot easier said than done. They never imagined it would be right beneath their feet.

One of the American commanders, Major General Dupuy, named the operation 'Crimp' to describe how he planned to block off escape routes to the north and south, then squeeze the Vietcong between them with a sweep through the area. Brigadier General Ellis 'Butch' Williamson was to take his 173rd Brigade through the north of the area while the Australians of 1 RAR were to block any escape to the south.

But the day before the assault, 1 Battalion Operations Officer Major John Essex-Clark flew low over the proposed landing zone (code-named 'June') and didn't like what he saw: there were no leaves on the ground from the surrounding trees. He suspected, rightly, that earth from recent work on defences had covered them. He raised his objections with the Allied forces' senior officers, but there was fierce opposition to changing the plans at such a late stage. It was only when Butch Williamson backed him up that they agreed to switch to another landing zone nearby. That decision almost certainly saved hundreds of Australian lives, as did taking the decision to attack the Ho Bo Woods in the field, not at the spy-ridden ARVN III Corps HQ in Saigon.

But it was no picnic. For a start, the troops were under constant fire soon after the first of the Hueys started landing men and equipment in the relocated landing zone (code-named 'March'). In fact, as mentioned earlier, a signal from Saigon, warning the Vietcong that Crimp was on, was intercepted minutes before they launched the attack. To make matters worse, the Aussies were being shelled by their own side. The main concentration of fire had crept to within 90 metres of the diggers before Essex-Clark—with a few choice phrases—managed to get the US artillery to stop firing.

And that wasn't the only screw-up. Just before the second wave of choppers went in, two American gunships started strafing Australians on the ground, thinking they were Vietcong hiding in the trees. It's as well that they weren't terribly good shots. Mistakes aside, the operation had followed the textbook. An artillery bombardment and air strike immediately before the ground troops went in should have had the Vietcong on the run. Unfortunately, they were reading a different script . . . their own.

The Vietcong went underground during the shelling and bombing, then—when the main body of 1 RAR arrived—they began popping up on all sides from trenches, tunnels and fox holes. By the time the headquarters and reserve element of 3 Field Troop—37 in all—touched down, they were putting up stiff resistance.

Sandy MacGregor vividly recalls the landing: 'Soon after I hit the ground, I bumped into the battalion commander, Lieutenant Colonel Alex Preece. There were shells exploding all round our ears. "What do you think of this?" he asked me. I said: "To be honest, I think I might lie down for a while." And I was only half joking. Some shrapnel landed a couple of feet from me and I picked it up. I remember being surprised at how bloody hot it was but I was glad I wasn't wearing it.

'I was interested in my own reaction to that situation, with bullets zipping around and great plumes of earth sprayed up into the sky where the shells hit. Anybody who tells you they don't feel fear when they're being shot at, mortared and shelled is either a liar or a lunatic. Fear is what keeps you alive; it's panic that gets you and your men killed.'

Luck comes into it too. Captain Ken Bade, an artillery officer and Sandy's best mate in Vietnam, was killed there. Ken was forward artillery observation officer with B Company under Major Ian McFarlane. B Company were the first in and they were probably the first to see the artillery shells and clusters of grenades attached to wires dangling from trees. But they didn't see the booby trap hidden in a bush that went off just as Ken was walking past. He took it full in the chest and he died there as Captain Peter Arnison, McFarlane's second-in-command, comforted him.

This was the first taste of real action for most of 3 Field Troop. The distant shots and muffled explosions they'd almost got used to were now a lot closer, and they were in the middle of them. Sparrow Christie still has a picture of a dead Vietcong soldier; it was the first dead body he and most of his mates had seen. They reacted with typical youthful bravado.

'We were walking past and he was just lying there. We cheered and laughed and shouted a lot of stuff about him being the first of many, and all that,' recalls Sparrow. 'Then about 20 metres further on we had to walk past a dead Aussie. It was this big red-headed fellow I used to drink with in the Railway Hotel. That jerked me back into gear.'

They needed to be on their toes. There was a Vietnamese village at the heart of 1 RAR's operation and there were women, children and old people running around in little groups. There was no way of knowing whether they were enemy or innocent civilians. It seems hardly likely that they were Vietcong but women and children were often found carrying weapons and grenades and old people were frequently used as decoys. The Aussies were under constant sniper fire and skirmishes would break out as knots of Vietcong appeared as if from nowhere. With the area laced with booby traps, which the engineers had to deal with, it was a desperate time for everyone. It's one thing to dismantle a familiarly constructed bomb in the relative calm of an army training camp; it's another to be confronted with a home-made, but no less deadly, piece of hardware while war rages around your ears.

However, it could have been worse. The assault had caught the Vietcong with their pants down—partly because they didn't know exactly when the Allies were coming; partly because they didn't anticipate where they were going to land. They'd been half-ready, sure, but the last-minute changes of plan meant they were taken by surprise and partially outflanked, with their positions set up to provide cross-fire over the original drop zone. Hundreds of men would have been wiped out if Essex-Clark hadn't insisted on landing elsewhere.

However, the Vietcong still had one surprise up their sleeve. When the infantrymen reached Landing Zone June, the clearing which had originally been earmarked as the landing zone, they set about securing the perimeter so that it could be crossed in safety. The area was a mixture of low scrub and dense bush, with a plantation of trees next to the landing zone. It was well defended with booby traps, from trip-wired grenades to clusters of vicious metal or bamboo spikes hidden under grass in holes in the ground.

When some of the infantrymen reached Landing Zone June, they came under machine-gun fire. They picked the worst option they could have—seeking cover in a washed-out gully beside a track. To their cost, they'd gone to ground right under the noses of Vietcong in a machine-gun post hidden in a hollowed-out mound of earth. They only realised their mistake when a couple of them were shot, virtually at point blank range. But in the confusion no one knew where the shots had come from.

The area was supposed to be secure. There should not have been any enemy troops within range. Two medics crawled in to treat the wounded. They were both shot and killed before the Aussies, realising the shots were coming from the narrow slits in the mound of earth, returned fire. That deadly mound, which looked for all the world like an anthill, was the key to one of the greatest secrets of the Vietnam War. But all it represented to the soldiers in the gully was a threat to their lives, so a couple of grenades made it safe until it could be properly investigated.

Meanwhile, Alex Preece anticipated a counterattack, so that first night the troop set about consolidating their positions. As darkness fell, they could hear the sounds of the Vietcong below them. They expected there to be tunnels and they knew the Vietcong were in them. But had they known the extent of the tunnel system, or what it contained, none of them would have slept that night.

The next day Sandy was called up to look at the mound of earth from which the two medics had been shot. This was definitely a job for engineers.

'We gained entry by blowing open a hole and, sure enough, found spent cartridges, presumably from the bullets our four lads had copped,' he recalls. 'But we also discovered a tunnel leading away from the position, and disappearing far under the ground.'

Obviously, that was how the snipers had got into their position. But how had they got into the tunnel? The standard practice when any tunnels were discovered was to blow smoke down them, using a device called the Mighty Mite, then look for the telltale signs of other entrances. Once the entrances were secured, tear gas was blown down to flush out any enemy troops and then the tunnel entrances were destroyed with explosives. But two months earlier, in his initial report, Sandy had highlighted how inadequate this was and had suggested a radical new approach to 'tunnel warfare', as it would become known.

'I suggested then that, after smoking the tunnels out and pumping tear gas down them, rather than seal them up, we should blow fresh air down them, and send men wearing gasmasks down to investigate,' says Sandy. 'After the tunnel had been cleared, it could then be destroyed. We had developed a tunnel search kit, complete with miner's-lamp-style lights for our hats, just for such an occasion. This would be our first chance to put it to proper use.'

Three Field Troop blew smoke into the tunnel, using the Mighty Mite, and Sandy divided the men into smaller subunits of twos and threes and sent them off to investigate. It was Dennis Ayoub who found the first entrance, which was booby-trapped. They'd already had a lot of experience with Vietcong booby traps, so he had a good look around and spotted that there were lines running from the entrance to hand grenades in nearby trees. The idea was that if anyone opened the entrance, the lines would pull the pins of the grenades and . . . ka-boom! However, the safety pins were still in most of the booby traps, another sure sign the Vietcong hadn't expected visitors just then. Bruce Lauder and Dennis Ayoub actually cleared eighteen booby traps (mainly grenades) all interconnected and designed to go off simultaneously.

Just to make sure the entrance wasn't booby-trapped on the inside too, Sandy sent Corporal Bill Gallagher and Sapper Barry Harford underground from the mound to check it out. It was clear, and that's when the tunnel entrance could be opened and the search could begin in earnest. Prior to this, the tunnels they had investigated had only been rat runs from underneath houses out to the safety of nearby paddy fields. But these entrances in the middle of the Ho Bo Woods were signs of something bigger and more complex, a fact that was confirmed when an infantryman found another part of the tunnel system by accident while he was digging a latrine several hundred metres away.

The troop discovered that the first tunnel ran right around the original landing zone to another mound with its gun overlooking the clearing. It was obvious then that if 1 RAR had landed there as planned, they'd have been the meat in a hot metal sandwich. Once they'd used the Mighty Mites to blow smoke, then tear gas, then fresh air down the tunnels, Sandy sent a couple of men down to investigate.

As a captured Vietcong document would later reveal (see Appendix A), these tunnels were no simple holes in the ground. Meticulous design, planning and construction went into them and the first obvious result of this was how hard it was to get in there. The entrance was deliberately narrow, there was a straight drop, then it could double back up, sometimes with a water trap, like the U-bend under a sink, to defeat any gas that might be pumped down there. Sometimes that water concealed nothing more than a potentially fatal dead end.

The tunnel might become a little wider and a bit higher... but it might not. There was no way of knowing until you crawled along and found out for yourself. There might be anterooms off to the side and trapdoors under the floor leading to... what? The first Tunnel Rats had no way of being sure what lay beyond the next corner or below the concealed entrance that their bayonet had found. And there were corners—lots of corners—designed to frustrate chemical attacks, mines and 'bangalores', bombs on the end of a long pole or pipe, designed to be slid under or through enemy defences before being detonated.

The Tunnel Rats could only be lightly armed at best: a bayonet to feel for booby traps and a pistol were all they had. A rifle would have been too cumbersome and, in any case, in such a confined space it would have deafened whoever fired it. Gasmasks were essential; the first thing they did on discovering a tunnel was to pump tear gas down it. Later, a pair of tunnel rats might be dragging a field telephone along to report their position and relay back to the surface what they were finding. But the worst thing was that they were venturing into the unknown. They had no idea who was down there and how many Vietcong there might be. They could only hope there weren't new and even more fiendish booby-traps that they hadn't encountered before.

But none of this was known before the first Aussies had gone into the tunnels. There was no standard operating procedure to follow, no training other than what they had devised themselves and no expectation of what they might find down there, for one very simple reason . . . the Australians of 3 Field Troop were the original Tunnel Rats, and they were going where no Allied soldiers had ever gone before.

# 10. THE FIRST TUNNEL RATS

There are two things that are significant about Operation Crimp—the strategic importance of the Ho Bo Woods tunnels and the role that 3 Field Troop played in investigating them. There have been claims and counterclaims but it is Sandy MacGregor's firm belief that Australians were the first to go down into the Vietcong tunnel systems and investigate them in any real way. Why? Firstly, if the Americans had been going down the tunnels, how come they never warned anyone about the dangers of oxygen depletion, a problem they would certainly have encountered?

Secondly, why was the general order to search all tunnels issued only *after* Operation Crimp?

'Let me go on the record—we were the original Tunnel Rats

and let those who have claimed the distinction for themselves prove otherwise,' says Sandy, who is quick to also commend the courage and resourcefulness of all the troops, Australian and American, who followed. Nevertheless, he couldn't be clearer: 3 Field Troop were the original Tunnel Rats.

That aside, what 3 Field Troop did and what they learned on Operation Crimp was incredible. In fact, they came close to changing the course of the Vietnam War that week in January 1966. If they had, it might well have changed history. They had gone to find and destroy the Saigon/Cho Lon/Gia Dinh political and military headquarters of the Vietcong. By the time they left, they knew they'd found it and were pretty sure they'd destroyed it. History shows that the former assumption was bang on while the latter was well off the mark.

The troop was in the Ho Bo Woods for six days on Crimp, but every day dawned to startling revelations, each of which was followed by even more amazing discoveries. They had three tasks. The first was to investigate the tunnels as fully as possible to discover what they were being used for. The second was to try to map the tunnel system so that they could work out its extent and, in an emergency, dig down to a soldier who might be trapped. The third, once they discovered what a treasure trove the tunnels were, was to recover everything they could—weapons, equipment and paper—all of which were invaluable for the Intelligence boys. But with the constant danger of men either collapsing in sections with foul air or coming face to face with the enemy, mapping the tunnels was the number one priority.

'I can remember we had some sort of telephone line we used to drag behind us so we could keep in contact,' recalls Sparrow Christie. 'Tommy Mason and I were down there and we'd gone as far as we could have gone. But there were branches off everywhere and I think Sandy had said just keep talking . . . tell us every move you make. Every time you come to a corner go to the right, just go to the right. And we had to ring back compass bearings.

'I came to one and thought I couldn't go on but I thought I'll just go a bit further, just go a bit further and I kept on going. Then I came across a lot of gear stacked in the tunnel. I was scrambling over the top of it. I came back and reported it on the telephone and then I had to go back again, 'cause I'd come to a dead end and there was a trapdoor out into the open. When I got back to the trapdoor I had to stand up inside the entrance tunnel and fire two shots into the closed trapdoor in rapid succession.

'The infantry were waiting to hear me and they fired two shots in reply. I had to say whether it was at nine o'clock or six o'clock or eight o'clock or whatever and from that they worked out where I was. The hairy part was waiting for the infantry to sweep through to me. Some of those forward

*An early shot (October 1965) of the base camp at Bien Hoa. Being very swampy, a first task was drainage—even then the drains wouldn't hold up without being reinforced.*

*With time the facilities at Bien Hoa grew to include better toilets and hot and cold running water.*

*Sandy's office, built from some of the timber taken from the Saigon wharves. It was the last building to go up at Bien Hoa and he got to work in it for less than ten days.*

*Sapper Les Colmer, lying down on the job, with Lance Corporal 'Blue' Hutton doing a radio watch. This part was okay—carrying the radios was the real chore.*

*Getting to the Rice Bowl area of Vo Dat and Vo Xu was a challenge. This is the main road into Vo Xu, which was cut in seven places within 100 metres. A few hours earlier these waters were a raging torrent.*

*Corporal Jack Fairweather (and others) carrying anything they could get their hands on to fill up the craters. In six hours this was a road ready to take 10th Division ARVN.*

*This 35-metre (120-foot) bridge on the way to Vo Xu had all its abutments blown and was cut at the 25-metre (80-foot) mark. A great field engineering feat that saved 24 hours of major construction time was to make it a 25-metre bridge.*

*Below: This diagram, copied from Sandy's original operational notes, shows the lower 25-metre (80-foot) crossing. The bridge was 'cut' with explosives and the concrete piers removed. The whole task took 6 hours and Sandy won a case of beer from his US Engineer boss.*

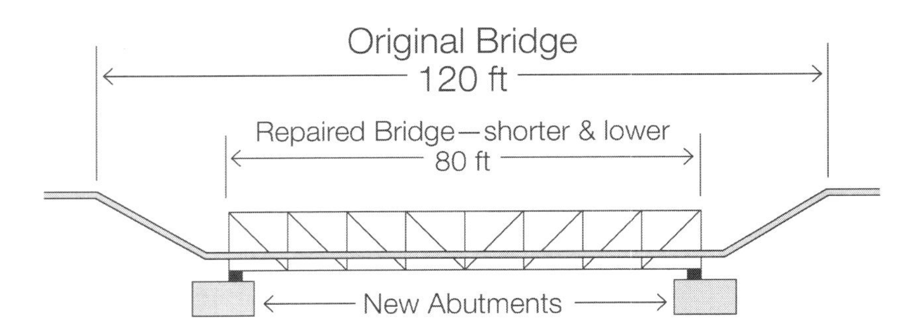

*A bridge was needed between Vo Xu and Mapu. The men were lucky to find three good trees and get a crane from RAEME.*

*The nearly completed 8-metre bridge using pierced steel plate as a decking.*

*Villagers from Vo Xu going to work in the rice fields—slowed down by a broken footbridge. Although of no strategic value, this bridge was rebuilt by 3 Field Troop under the 'Civic Action' program.*

*Sappers dig for mines found just outside the gates of Vo Xu. All roads were first checked using a mine detector.*

*A Chinook helicopter extracts a lightly bogged APC using a dozer's winch rope on Operation Marauder near the Cambodian border. There were seven more APCs to dig out.*

*One helicopter gunship stays up in the air to protect the slick of choppers picking up a load of Aussies on the Plain of Reeds. The operation near the Cambodian border had just finished and 3 Field Troop were on their way to Operation Crimp.*

*Time to snatch a brew and a bite, from left, Doug Sanderson, Bill Unmeopa, Dave Cook (rear) and Sandy Saunders.*

*The troop's first ever tunnel, found 50 kilometres to the east of the huge tunnel system discovered later. Staff Sergeant Laurie Hodge holds a rope tied to Sandy's ankles as Sandy cautiously probes the floor, walls and roof with a bayonet.*

*Sapper Dennis Ayoub near the enemy bunker—the hollowed-out mound with the bush on top, just above and to the left of his head—which started the tunnel search.*

*The enemy inside this bunker shot dead two soldiers and wounded two others. Sandy's men blew in the bunker, gaining access to the tunnel system, and began the historic tunnel search from there.*

*This area, originally intended to be used as the landing zone, was overlooked from the enemy bunker (the one with the bush on top shown on the previous page)—it would have been a killing field if plans hadn't been changed at the last minute.*

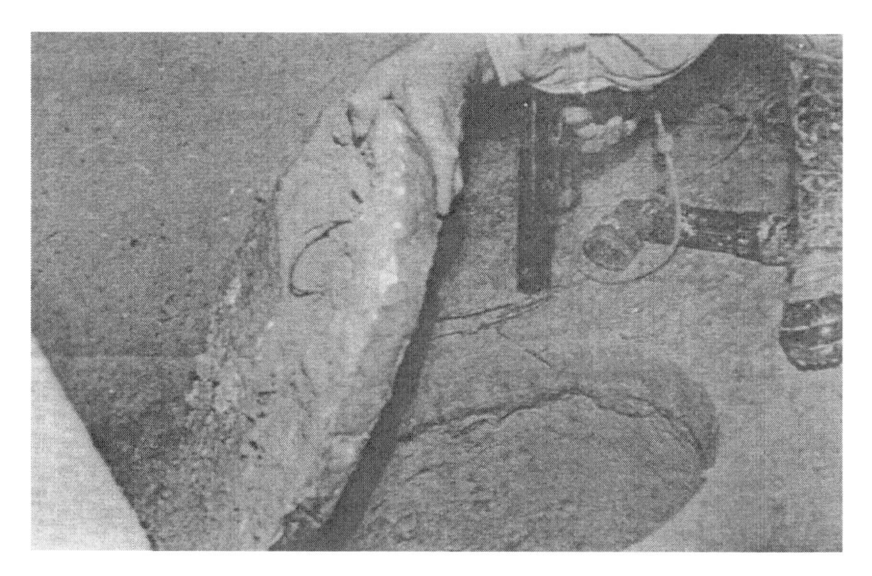

*A trapdoor, about 40 centimetres in diameter, within the tunnel complex. Beyond the trapdoor the tunnel goes vertically down for about 1 metre.*

*It was only after Operation Crimp that better tunnel equipment was developed, like the microphone, earphone, light and silenced pistol carried by this American engineer.*

*This hinged tunnel entrance is 40 centimetres square. It was about 10 metres from the enemy bunker and had 18 booby traps connected into the trees around the trapdoor.*

*Sapper Alan 'Sparrow' Christie looking through the sights of the Vietcong Russian Sniper rifle he recovered from the tunnels on Operation Crimp.*

*Sapper 'Barney' Barnett between a couple of Vietcong mortar rounds.*

*Two Vietcong fragmentation grenades—complete (right) and dismantled—made in the jungle. The top grenade uses a food tin as the outer casing and chunks of metal as the fragments.*

*Back in Bien Hoa airbase the equipment captured on Operation Crimp was put on display for the soldiers to admire.*

*Billy Coolburra and Snow Wilson—the 'twins' to whom Prime Minister Holt wanted to say hello. The picture is courtesy of Snow.*

*Early days at the sandhills in Vung Tau—three dozers worked around the clock for a month levelling areas for occupation.*

*The water point at Vung Tau was made by dozers pushing sand to a mound and then deepening the waterhole with a drag line.*

*The first Task Force Water Point at Nui Dat was built in the engineer location—note the 10,000-gallon water bladders.*

*The third camp set up at Vung Tau, just before the troop was moved. These are the showers they were ordered to leave behind for officers of 1 ALSG but which were mysteriously 'booby-trapped' and had to be destroyed.*

scouts have been known to shoot first and ask questions later. Anyway, they came and caught up with me. I could hear them above and they could hear me below. The engineers with them found the entrance, which was attached to booby-trapped grenades in the trees designed to go off when it was opened. I'm glad we didn't open the trapdoor. Then we got all this gear out; and from there on we got more and more gear.'

Sandy MacGregor says looking back, it felt like they were there for a month rather than six days, so much was happening. On the first day, the demolition team attached to A Company searched and destroyed a tunnel which was 25 metres long and had a sleeping bay for about five people. There was nothing particularly unusual in that. About twenty 'domestic' trench, bunker and tunnel systems were searched and destroyed. They also came across some home-made bombs and grenades set as booby traps.

On day 2 the B Company demolition team searched a bunker system under a house and found a room about 2.5 metres long by 2 metres wide by 1.5 metres high, full of weapons, ammunition, mortar shells, grenades, clothing and documents. This is probably the pile of gear Sparrow Christie referred to, and it created quite a stir.

The trapdoor entrance was only 50 centimetres square and was hidden under a layer of dirt.

They also had to deal with more booby traps, including

vicious barbed steel spikes in the ground, one of which went through Terry Bradbury's foot. The D Company demolition team searched bunkers and tunnels starting from houses and finishing in open exits in the field—one was 45 metres long.

On day 3 the team investigated a lot more tunnel systems. Only one of the initial searches turned up anything of interest—but it more than made up for the other disappointments. Again, the tunnel began under a house, but this time instead of weapons, they found a typewriter, medical supplies and documents. The C Company demolition team blew smoke and tear gas through after that, then, when no one came out, blew up the tunnel entrances to seal it.

The A Company demolition team found a home-made rifle, a sewing machine and a radio in a tunnel under a house. One Vietcong was hit by gunfire and disappeared down a hole in the ground. The hole was tear-gassed then a grenade was dropped down it. The assumption then was that the enemy would have died. Later discoveries revealed he could have gone even further underground.

'We found sewing machines and the rolls of material, weapons and a makeshift hospital, living quarters and a cooking area,' says Mick. 'You can't put the magnitude of it into words. You just think of a tunnel as a tunnel, no rooms or anything like that running off it.'

The D Company demolition team found a radio and an ID

card in another tunnel. A whole squad of Vietcong were seen in the same area—and then, just as quickly, they disappeared. When the tunnel system was found, webbing, grenades, magazines and anti-aircraft gun sights were retrieved. This may have been the same tunnel search that Snow Wilson recalls.

'There was a team of us, Meggsie Dennis, Sparrow Christie, Tex Cotter, Barry Harford, Billy Unmeopa, Billy Gallagher, Tommy Mason and myself, searching out the tunnels. While we were down there we went from the level we were on down another level and found this cache of 12.7 mm Chicom anti-aircraft guns, rice, weapons and heaps and heaps of paperwork. We were just pushing this stuff up out of the ground for about an hour. There were four complete Chicom anti-aircraft guns, two of them had anti-aircraft sights, there was one incomplete one that I think was missing its breech block but everything else was there. That was our first really big weapons cache. Then the next day, as I recall, we really started clearing those areas and we were spending a long time underground.'

The previous day John Cotter and Dennis Ayoub had found a blue bag down in the main tunnel, but they got into trouble due to lack of air and withdrew, leaving the bag where it was. When they went back two days later, the bag had gone, which confirmed something they already suspected—the Vietcong were coming back into the tunnels after the engineers had left them.

The D Company team had a Vietnamese dog and handler allotted to them. They were called forward when a trapdoor was lifted and Vietnamese voices were heard underground. They confirmed there were Vietcong in the tunnel and, since they couldn't coax them out, they blew up the entrance. The team reckoned then that they had trapped about eight Vietcong down there. It now seems likely the Vietcong had just found another exit in that underground city.

The South Vietnamese soldiers were loath to enter the tunnels under any circumstances and, judging by Sandy MacGregor's records, 3 Field Troop were more impressed with the dog than its handler. 'The dog can most definitely indicate whether there are people down the tunnels and in fact is keen to track the victims down,' he wrote. 'The handler on the other hand is not so eager . . .'

The next day, day 4, saw the engineers find several trapdoors and tunnels and once again they could hear Vietnamese voices. Corporal Bob Bowtell, the leader of the B Company demolition team, decided to investigate. Bob was tough, disciplined and well liked by the men. At 32, he was older than most of the troop. And, being ex-infantry, he saw himself as a bit more of a soldier too. He was fiercely loyal to the men in his charge and had recently backed one of them in an argument with Sandy MacGregor. Determined as ever to keep a tight rein on things, Sandy barred him from the next two operations. To a man like Bob Bowtell, sitting in camp while the rest of the troops were out in the field was a worse punishment than solitary confinement or a 100-mile route march. Crimp was his first operation after he'd done his penance.

Bob was a big, rangy bloke, about six foot two and, like any good NCO, he led from the front. That meant that when they discovered the narrow entrance, he felt he had to be the one to go down. Even though it was a tight fit for his broad shoulders, Bob squeezed himself into the narrow passage and round a U-bend into a chamber. By the time he realised it was a dead end and there was no air, it was too late. He collapsed, as did his offsider Sapper Peter Cachia. Peter can't remember how he got out, but he did.

'I was astonished to find in my records that the tunnel entrance Bob squeezed himself into was only 16 inches by 11 inches,' says Sandy MacGregor. Now, it is one thing for a big man to wriggle through a tight tunnel. It's another to push or even pull the same bulk upwards through the same space when it is limp and lifeless. Being one of the smallest men in the troop, Sparrow Christie was sent down to help him out while the others, including infantrymen, dug frantically to widen the hole.

'He was just a dead weight,' Sparrow recalls. 'Whenever I tried to push or pull him, there was no movement—he just stuck in the vertical shaft. So I started digging around him with my bayonet. Then, when I broke through to the space beyond him all this stale air came up and I nearly passed out.'

Sparrow was dragged to the surface and when Peter Ash went down in his place he almost suffered the same fate as Bob. Peter passed out completely and was dragged back up. Sparrow recovered sufficiently to help Peter Ash to the field dressing station. He was still unaware that Bob was dead by the time they got him out of the tunnel. He assumed that he'd been rescued. Bob's death stunned the whole troop.

For Sandy MacGregor, this first death under his command was a particularly bitter realisation of the cruelties of war: 'I have asked myself if Bob was trying to prove something when he went down that hole; if he was trying to show that I couldn't afford to leave him out of my plans again. But he was a professional—not given to risking his life just to prove a petty point. He was a brave man who took the toughest jobs himself, leading by example. If it had to be done, he had to be the one to do it. He lost his life because he was a good soldier, not because he was trying to be a hero.'

Snow Wilson, who still felt Bob's loss decades later, cannot praise the man highly enough: 'When you think about it, it's a fairly big thing in a 20-year-old's life. Bob Bowtell was a section corporal and I regarded him as a friend of mine. He used to make me money when we were in Borneo. I can't shuffle cards but I love playing poker. Bob loved playing poker but couldn't afford to play because he was a very good family man and sent all his money home. So he used to sit behind me and when it was my turn to deal he'd shuffle the cards.

'I'd deal them, play, and if I won I'd buy him a beer. That way he had the best of both worlds, he could sit and watch the poker, enjoy himself, have a couple beers and still have money to send home. Bob was, in my book, a perfect choice for sergeant but he volunteered to go to South Vietnam as a section corporal. He'd had six or seven years in the infantry, where he was a section commander, and transferred to engineers as a corporal. He went to Borneo with 1 Field Squadron and performed magnificently. He was respected by everybody that I can think of.'

Snow believes that Bob was motivated by nothing more than sheer professionalism to go down that tunnel. 'Bob Bowtell was a totally professional soldier and was always prepared to take the necessary risk. I think he was cut out to be a regimental sergeant major. He was a fantastic soldier.'

This was the first and only death in the platoon and for the raw young soldiers of 3 Field Troop it was a situation for which they were unprepared, strange as that may seem in armed combat. A mixture of bravado and denial made it hard for the message to sink in that one of their own had gone. Even by the next morning Sparrow Christie still had no idea that his rescue attempt had been in vain. Gulping down a hurried breakfast with the lads he made a joke of his own attempts to save Bob.

'Wake up, Sparrow,' Snow Wilson said. 'Bob's dead!' It was a shock for Sparrow and it would turn out to be a rude awakening for the whole army. As 3 Field Troop would discover, Bob Bowtell's death was almost inevitable; they were going into uncharted territory developing their survival techniques as they went. You have to make mistakes if you're going to learn from them.

Bob Bowtell's death was sheer bad luck. The tunnel he went into was a dead end and when he used up the oxygen, his own body was blocking air that would have kept him alive. But there was still danger for the men who burrowed away in longer tunnels, ever further, ever deeper, when they too began passing out. Despite the fact that there was no room to turn they were all dragged back to the surface, usually after the troop had used the Mighty Mite to blast more fresh air down to them.

Les Colmer had at least one rescue to his credit: 'Barry Harford and I, we were both from Broken Hill, we went in and got Billy Gallagher when he went too far and he got all funny and had to be pulled out.' In fact, Barry Harford was with Gallagher when Gallagher passed out. Les Colmer went in to help Barry, then Sandy told Barry to come out and sent in Dennis Ayoub. It was a long time before Billy was brought back to the surface, but he began to recover as soon as he reached fresh air and he was fine in twenty-four hours or so.

Sandy had been sending the men down in twos, but even then, on at least one occasion, both of them had to be rescued when they ran out of air. So he organised some teams of three and even four, with the tail-enders paying out telephone wire as their mates negotiated the twists and turns of the tunnel. The man in front would check for booby traps as they went along, the second man would support him and stay in touch with the surface by phone. The guys at the back would sit at the tighter corners, making sure the cable didn't snag.

All the time they'd be talking to their section commander on the surface, who'd be using their reports to try to work out at ground level where they were so that they could be dug out from above if necessary. The men up top also tried to draw maps of the tunnel system as they described it.

'I was the tail-end Charlie, sitting in the dark with no torch, no phone or nothing when the guys I was working with—Barry Harford and Tommy Mason—went very quiet,' Snow Wilson recalls. 'I went back and reported it and MacGregor said he already knew and he was sending a new team in to get them out because we'd been underground a couple of hours at the time. I said, 'Bullshit, I know exactly where they are and I know how to get to them. I'm going to see what's wrong. '

'So I shot down there and here's the first of them, Tommy, just sitting there giggling and chuckling and carrying on. I thought he was pissed, I really did. I thought he'd found a rice wine stash or some bloody thing. Then I realised he was gassed so I grabbed him by the scruff of the neck and dragged him the 50 or 60 bloody odd metres back and stuck him out through the hole.'

Tex Cotter went down next and he and Snow brought Barry Harford out. 'I pushed him out of the hole and then I thought "Well, I haven't got the excuse to stay in here any longer, I better go out and face MacGregor." He wasn't particularly impressed when I got out, but luckily, as I was taking the gasmask off, I bumped into a couple of blokes,' says Snow. 'I was still pumped up from dragging the lads back and I said, "Why don't you get out of me fucking road?" Trouble was, the two blokes were Major Essex-Clark and Colonel Preece. Essex-Clark said, "If I thought you could see me, son, I'd charge you." All I could say was "Ooops, sorry, sir." So much for being a hero!'

Snow Wilson had good reason to want to make sure his team-mates survived; he'd lost a friend and a mentor and that wound wasn't going to heal any time soon.

# 11. THE UNDERGROUND ARMY

On the same day that Bob Bowtell died, the C Company demolition team used the dog team to confirm Vietcong activity in a tunnel which was later blown up. That night they could hear the sound of the Vietcong trying to dig themselves out. They tried to dig down to them and the entrances were opened and tear gas was blown through, but nobody came out. On days 5 and 6 all the company demolition teams were still finding amazing amounts of arms, equipment and documents, especially from the larger rooms they had found.

And despite Bob's death, the men were still keen to go down the tunnels . . . especially if there was a prize at the end of it. Sparrow Christie ended up with a Czech snipers' rifle after chasing a wounded Vietcong into a tunnel.

'The infantry had shot him but he was getting away and he dived down this hole. The grunts said tunnels were engineers' work, down you go. We got down there and there was a bit of blood—you know, he obviously hadn't been shot bad, he'd only been nicked. We chased him and I used an Owen gun—the old Second World War one with the magazine on top—which was totally ridiculous because if you fired it in a confined space like that you'd be deaf for a month. But it made you feel confident with that much firepower.

'We got down and we were chasing him. I could hear him in front. I was wearing a lamp like a miner's helmet light with dry cell batteries but you weren't game to switch it on. It made you too good a target. But what you could see in the dark was phosphorus. They had that there so they could run along and they didn't need lights. They'd just lay it along in the corners. So you only switched your light on when you had to—if you come to a trapdoor or a dead end or something.

'Anyway, I never actually saw him but I could hear him and he wasn't all that far in front of me. Eventually I came to the rifle. It was in a leather case and I thought, "What do I do: take the spoils or chase him?" I knew some bastard would come behind me and grab it. So I said, fuck it. I didn't have communications back to the surface or anything. So I just dragged it back and I got out and I said he got away but I got this. And the grunts were OK about it. They said a trophy was better than a kill any day.'

Barney Barnett was less sanguine when he turned a corner in a tunnel and came face to face with a pair of piercing eyes. 'It was one of the better frights of my life,' he says. 'Picture this: a 6-foot drop down the tunnel, a 70-foot crawl along and, I might add, blood at the entrance. Right turn, left turn, up a half a dozen steps into a hut. When I got out the infantry called us away to another hut which had a concealed room under it with a store full of 81 mm mortars, guns and ammo. To help spin out our own explosives, I took a couple of mortars to use for demolition of the other tunnel and then Sandy Saunders and I blew the whole store. We went back to the previous tunnel, this time down the other end. Down the steps and a short crawl dragging the mortars. With my torch and pistol I didn't have enough hands.

'I came round a corner and all I saw were two eyes looking at me. In the dark with my mind racing, my first thought was "Jesus, there's a Vietcong round the corner." When I had stopped shaking I put the pistol around the corner, followed by the torch. Then I realised the eyes belonged to a dog that was growling at me, and it was coming right from his arse end. I gave him the first round through the chest and he turned straight on his back, four legs stiff in the air.

'Then I got the shits and gave him the other eight rounds and grabbed him by the tail and dragged him upstairs. I yelled out to the boys, "It's only me, don't shoot." Needless to say, I had a couple of SLRs [self-loading rifles] looking down at me. They thought I'd been blueing with a Vietcong.'

It was difficult work down there. Apart from the twists and turns of the access tunnels, which would have trapdoors, possibly booby-trapped, every 20 metres or so, there was the fact that the Aussies were being burned on the hands and neck by the tear gas they'd pumped in at the beginning. And it was hard to imagine that there were no creepy-crawlies waiting underground to inflict some other pain on the invaders of their domain. Fortunately, apart from Barney Barnett's dog, there was little wildlife in the tunnels.

'Once you were down there it wasn't too bad, I suppose,' says Sandy Saunders. 'You know all this rubbish you hear about spiders, snakes and all that crap, you very seldom struck anything like that. The tunnels were pretty clean because the Vietcong had to live down there too. But the main thing I think was you never knew what was going on. You were just in your own little world and you never knew how long you were down there. You lost a sense of time.'

Time and distance lend enchantment (and a little drama) to most stories but Sandy MacGregor conducted interviews with the men after they finished their stints underground. They are the men's own descriptions of what they did and how they felt, recorded when the incidents were still fresh in their minds.

'The first time I had to go down was into the bunker

which the Vietcong had used to kill a couple of our fellows,' said Bill Gallagher who, in fact, was the first man to go down the tunnels. 'I was scared there was somebody still there and prior to going down we looked through a slit. We could see some webbing and I thought there might have been someone down there with this gear.

'I was cautious at first and didn't venture too far. I went only to where I could see the gear and examine the tunnel leading off from it. Then I came out to get a piece of cordage to tie to the gear and pull it out. With the webbing out, I went further. I kept thinking there might be someone down there around the corner but I just went through and checked it out. We then found more gear so I sent Sapper Lauder to sit at the entrance to the tunnel itself and watch up the tunnel while I got all the other gear out.'

Asked how fast he thought a Vietnamese, with a rifle and equipment, could move in the tunnels and whether he thought they would wear their equipment, or carry it, Bill said, 'Twice as fast as we can. Firstly, they would know where they were going, and then, being much smaller than we are, they can move faster. In many parts of the tunnel they could wear their equipment but they would have to take it off at the corners and trapdoors. I think they would carry it.'

The levels of courage some of the men of 3 Field Troop displayed were remarkable. They were going where no (Western) man had gone before, not knowing what to expect when they got down there, and finding equipment that suggested these tunnels were still very much active.

'You're apprehensive, once you get down the entrance shaft, out of sight of the outside light,' Tex Cotter said. 'You go along and think all kinds of things. What's up ahead? Who is there? But after about 10 or 15 minutes I settled down a bit. And next day was no problem.'

Bruce Lauder was much the same: 'I felt a bit scared at first. You get a bit frightened with no experience at this sort of thing. However, after a while you gain confidence in yourself and in your mates who are in there with you. However, you need to be careful not to get overconfident. In any new tunnel you must be very cautious.'

So imagine how these men felt when soldiers started dropping like flies as they were overcome by fumes and lack of oxygen. It takes a brave man to go into a hole in the ground knowing his mates could be at death's door and the same fate could await him. Bill Gallagher, the first to go down the tunnels at Cu Chi, was also the first to need rescuing.

'I started to become a bit drowsy,' said Bill. 'I began to realise what was happening and I knew I'd have to get out straightaway or become unconscious. You feel it affecting you and I knew what was happening straightaway. When I turned around I started to move faster and my breathing became heavy and I started gasping.

'The thought in my mind at that moment was to get back

as far as I could . . . so someone would come to my aid. Otherwise, if I didn't reach C* before I lost power to think, I could go past C towards V. You see, there was a vertical shaft going down at point C. We had not been down there and I didn't know what was down there. I would not have been in any state to do anything for myself.

'Apparently I blacked out before I got to C. I must have been crawling while semi-conscious because I was nowhere near the T-junction when I lost reason. The next thing I remember I saw lights and I was being pulled out of the tunnel at A. I was then taken back to hospital.'

Alan Tugwell was with him and he too was affected by the fumes: 'I entered the tunnel at point A with Corporal Gallagher and crawled along to point C,' he said. 'On the way to point D . . . I felt a bit drowsy and called out to Corporal Gallagher and told him I had to go back because of the fumes. I was trying to hurry yet slow my movements down to keep my breathing slow. I started gasping and then saw light at the entrance of the tunnel, where I received medical treatment.'

With Sapper Tugwell struggling, Bruce Lauder realised Bill Gallagher probably needed help. 'I crawled to point C where I found Corporal Gallagher,' said Bruce. 'He was unconscious. I tried to pull him back but I found I couldn't do it. I was

---

* These letters relate to the map on page ix.

starting to feel groggy so I came back out and received medical attention. I found him slightly past C on his way to V. He had just passed the T-junction. I could hear him breathing. I knew the noise was not coming from my own gasmask so I stopped breathing to listen for him. By using the torch I found him hunched up in the tunnel slightly past C. He still had his light clutched in his hand, his revolver was on the ground in front of him and he was still in the crawling position when I found him.

'He was unconscious and breathing heavily so I tried to pull him out. I reached the junction and started to feel groggy myself and I felt like going to sleep. I knew then I had to get out and that if I didn't get out, no one would know what had happened to Bill. I can only have pulled him about five feet. It was too hard because the tunnel was so small and he was so limp. When I dragged him by the feet I saw his gasmask come off his face. I knew then I could not do anything so I got out. The smoke was fierce. Smoke and tear gas.

'I think we went down two levels before reaching C and at C we went down again. Generally at a major corner the tunnel goes down another flight and still keeps twisting. It is hard to see far with the torch as there are so many corners. We hadn't gone through any trapdoors but we did pass a section of the tunnel where the walls had caved in a bit and it just left a small opening to crawl over. It didn't look as if the cave-in had occurred long ago, but the floor itself had packed down hard where it had a lot of use.'

Barry Harford also went down with Les Colmer to rescue Bill Gallagher: 'I first went down from A to C to help Corporal Gallagher after Sapper Lauder came out. I came out affected by gas and spent the night in the RAP,' Barry said. 'We found him at the T-junction and had a lot of trouble getting him out. He was lying on his stomach. We had to sit him up and turn him because he was so limp and his gasmask kept coming off. We put that back on again. It kept coming off because we were moving him, plus the fact that he was very sweaty. He was perspiring quite a lot and his breathing was heavy. The rubber was just slipping off his face.

'At that stage I think we had been down there about 20 to 25 minutes. And I would say he must have been unconscious for at least 10 minutes before we reached him. We worked out a little system to move him along the tunnel. Crawling on my knees, I had him on his back with his knees tucked up on his chest. Sapper Colmer was in front of me, facing me and lifting under the Corporal's arms. But we could only take him a few feet at a time.

'We worked together and got him to the change in level. At this hole we had a lot of trouble. Colmer was very tired—he had all the weight in the front. He had to bend over to take it. Sapper Colmer went out and Sapper Cotter came down. At this stage we got a rope down. We had him sitting backwards to the hole, head looking up. We put the rope under his arms—it was the only way we could tie him. His head jammed as we pulled and his mask came off again. We could not get underneath him to lift. The rope didn't help much at all.

'Sapper Ayoub came down to help and I was very tired. Sappers Ayoub and Cotter pulled Corporal Gallagher on down the next straight portion, and here the rope did help. I believe I stayed down another 20 to 25 minutes before we got him out.'

Claustrophobia and lack of oxygen weren't the only hazards. Remnants of the tear gas used to clear the tunnels also affected the sappers.

'The gas burns the exposed parts of the body. It's like having a sweaty fever,' Bill Gallagher said. 'The gas seems to stick to the walls and floor and as soon as exposed skin touches walls or floor it burns. I first went down with my sleeves up, but quickly rolled them down. Even if you didn't touch anything, it still burned. And on the back of the neck particularly. You get over this by putting something like a sweat rag around your neck. Then, about three days after being down the tunnel, all the skin from my hands peeled away as if I had a bad case of sunburn. We need some type of rubber glove which is skin tight so that you have full use of the hands.'

Barry Harford was another who suffered: 'After you came out of the tunnel and the sweat started to dry you could feel it burn. We used to wash our eyes with water from our water bottles,' he said. 'Another point is that everyone should have his own gasmask. It is no good having to borrow the mask of another chap who has just come up affected by gas . . . it means re-adjusting straps all the time.'

Barry Harford told Sandy MacGregor the air in the tunnel was hot and it was easier to breathe with his gasmask off: 'Apart from the smoky areas already described, it was easy to breathe. The air was good, clean and fresh. It was not musty and in fact the smell was like newly ploughed earth. I think that with no more gas or smoke coming down you could stay down indefinitely. Colmer and I stayed down four hours and forty minutes at one stage and apart from sweating I felt all right when I came up.'

Breathing was just part of the art of staying alive. There was the ever-present threat of an enemy down there. 'We could have walked straight into an ambush,' said Bill Gallagher. 'When you're crawling along you make a lot of noise. The enemy could easily have been sitting in ambush over a killing zone and we would have had no chance. But after we had been down a while the fear passed a little. This was especially true when we had been down three to three-and-a-half hours.'

Barry Harford agreed: 'I was a bit worried. I come from a mining town at Broken Hill but this was the first time I had ever been down a tunnel. I didn't know what to expect, but as time went on I gained confidence. I became more confident each time I went down.'

The engineers' detailed descriptions of the tunnels paint a picture of an inhospitable environment for Australians and Americans but a hugely practical system for the smaller, nimbler Vietnamese.

'It was approximately 2 feet 6 inches to 3 feet wide, maybe 3 feet in depth—much bigger than the main tunnel which is about 2 feet wide and about 2 feet 6 inches high in most places,' said Bill Gallagher, describing the tunnel at Point A. 'It gets smaller on turns and is very cramped when it goes down another flight. The hole itself is only about 2 feet 6 inches round and that does not give much room to change levels. They then change direction which makes it much harder, and if there is anybody waiting down there on that corner you are helpless.

'The vertical shafts go down about 3 feet and change direction and some shafts were even smaller than 2 feet 6 inches in diameter, about the same size as the trapdoors on the surface, which were about 16 inches by 13 or 14 inches.'

Barry Harford explained that they always went down the shafts feet first: 'You'd like to have a look first but it's not possible to get your head down far enough to see. There is a 3-foot drop. It is easier to get out again if you go down feet first. Sapper Mason once got stuck going down headfirst.'

They also realised that these tunnels were no hurried or

temporary construction: 'It looked as if they spent some time digging this tunnel. The sides were not really rough. There were good surfaces on it and they had really made a job of it. Some parts could have been made for a special reason. We found places which sloped up and down and one which was about 4 feet high. Otherwise the average height was 2 feet 6 inches to 3 feet.

'There were quite a few passing bays and on the main tunnel there were quite a few offshoots where you could slip in to let a man pass. These are about 30 centimetres across by 40 centimetres high. Most of the tunnel was in pretty hard clay. In a couple of places I tried to stick a bayonet into the walls and floor but it would not go in more than an inch or two. The soil packs as hard as cement. When crawling along the floor it takes skin off everywhere. I lost skin from my knees and elbows. The floor had packed down hard and it looked as if it has been used extensively. Some parts I crawled through and came out with mud all over everything. It is quite damp in spots.'

Booby traps were a constant concern above ground so the engineers were right to be wary of them in the tunnels. However, yet again it seems the Vietcong had not expected Allied troops to follow them underground.

'There were pegs in the side of the wall to which they could have attached trip wires and at one place we found a vine halfway up the wall,' said Snow Wilson. 'It came down, crossed the floor and up the other wall and back into the earth. We didn't know if it was growing there or had been put there. The only place we found booby traps was at a side exit where a piece of wire was connected to the trapdoor. The wire was connected with a little peg under the trapdoor. The wire went through the dirt but it didn't have anything to do with the trapdoor.

'Even so, you didn't want to open the trapdoor from below, just in case. So we found it from the trapdoor . . . connected to two grenades, but the pins weren't prepared for firing. We lifted the trapdoor and nothing happened. When we found trapdoors in the tunnel, first of all we would put the torch close to the trapdoor and have a careful look for wires. The trapdoors fit very neatly and it is difficult to see a wire. Next, a corner of the trapdoor was raised slightly and a hand inserted underneath to feel for wires. Having found no wires the lid was taken off.'

The sappers were asked how they felt about going down again after Bob Bowtell had died and others had collapsed.

'It wasn't too bad as we virtually knew what had caused the accidents,' Bruce replied. 'However, you look out for these things and take care not to make the same mistakes.'

Snow Wilson reckoned they'd been lucky: 'After the accidents we worked for two days before striking gas again. We got our confidence back in these two days and we were all right when we next met gas.'

Two other significant issues came up as a result of this

unique and untried form of warfare. The first was that the men generally weren't properly equipped for tunnel searches. The ideal kit for a Tunnel Rat was a bayonet in one hand—for digging and testing for booby traps and trapdoors—and a pistol for dealing with the enemy in the other, plus a miner's lamp on the helmet. The trouble was that handguns were not general issue to lower ranks and Sandy MacGregor had to source them where he could.

'When he went into the tunnels the first time, there were two pistols in the troop and he had to beg, borrow and steal additional pistols,' says Warren Lennon, who would later take over as the Officer Commanding 1 Field Squadron. 'The concept of crawling through a tunnel was pretty horrible. So he learnt a lot of lessons and the information was passed on to us. Sandy had done most of the research there by experience, but we continued to improve on the personal equipment that was used and it was great.'

By the time they got themselves properly organised, there were four teams of six engineers, each attached to an infantry company, and they had men underground in shifts from dawn until dusk. With new procedures developed on the fly, new challenges faced and overcome, and the first death among their immediate comrades, when the order to leave Cu Chi came through, the Australian troops had learned more in a week about themselves and their enemy than some soldiers discover in an entire tour of duty.

Besides all the tunnel work going on within the companies' tactical area of responsibility, the major tunnel system was being searched all week. They had investigated tunnels for 700 metres in one direction and 500 metres across that line. They still had no idea how far the tunnels extended but had taken out truckloads of equipment and documents, including photographs of the Vietcong's foreign advisors and a hit list of political and military figures in Saigon whom the Vietcong wanted to assassinate.

'I'd be very surprised if some of the Vietcong papers returned to the Vietnamese by the USA in July 1993, as part of the two countries' reconciliation over US troops missing in action, weren't from the half ton extracted from the tunnels under Ho Bo Woods,' says Sandy.

But had they destroyed the Vietcong's command HQ for the Saigon area? The day before the operation ended and they were pulled out, Les Colmer and Barry Harford had gone further down the main tunnel than anyone had ever been when they found a large trapdoor. They carefully checked it for booby traps, then pulled it open. It led down to a third level. However, to their alarm, they could hear ticking. Les and Barry decided to retreat while they still could. They called back to report their find and Sandy MacGregor told them to leave it.

It was already late in the day and although they were underground, they were well out of the battalion perimeter.

It was decided by battalion HQ to blow the tunnels at the extremities, to prevent the enemy from coming into the battalion position at night. They could continue to search the tunnels outside the perimeter later in the operation. The next day while they were searching the tunnels within the battalion perimeter, the Americans decided to wrap the operation up and pull out.

The engineers of 3 Field Troop only went back down the tunnels to line them with explosives and bags of tear gas crystals. Their intention was solely to destroy the tunnels as best they could and leave those parts that they couldn't destroy as uninhabitable as possible. They didn't find out what was beneath that trapdoor until many years later. The Americans assumed they had already found the Vietcong headquarters and destroyed it, but it was just a tiny part of a larger system which ran for 300 kilometres.

In fact, beyond the trapdoor that Les and Barry found was the military headquarters of the southern command of the Vietcong. And at the other end of the search area, they were just as close to discovering the Vietcong's political HQ. The Vietcong hadn't expected the Allies to follow them into the tunnels—more evidence, if you need it, that the Aussies were the first to go underground—which is why they left all the equipment and documents that were captured.

The Vietcong had been ordered not to attack the soldiers who entered the tunnel system, so as not to arouse suspicions about how strategically vital it was and how many of them were hiding down there. But had Barry and Les gone through that last trapdoor, they would certainly have been killed and it would have been all on. The Vietcong political and military leaders interviewed by TV journalist Chris Masters on his program *Page One* said as much. The Vietcong had pulled back as far as they could without abandoning important installations. The next step would have meant bloody close-quarters fighting which the Allies would probably have won, but at a terrible cost.

Would it have changed the course of history? The Vietcong planned the Tet Offensive of 1968 from those tunnels. Ten years later they launched the final assault on Saigon from there, by which time the network had grown from 300 to 600 kilometres. But, more to the point, they would have suffered terrible military, political and logistical blows if the Allies had discovered the full extent of the tunnels, not to mention the crushing effect it would have had on their morale.

The Vietcong military leaders interviewed claimed that they had 5000 men down there at various times, some of whom didn't see the light of day for six months at a stretch. If 3 Field Troop had been allowed to continue for another couple of days, they would have had some idea of the size and complexity of the underground city and it would have been destroyed. Would that have led to the capitulation of

Hanoi? It's debatable, but the US decision to pull out led only, ultimately, to the fall of Saigon.

There aren't many, if any, Vietnamese survivors from the Cu Chi tunnels still alive—the war took many of them and age has caught up with the rest—but the importance of the tunnel system is revealed in a captured document which is basically a 'how to' training booklet on tunnel planning, building and operations (see Appendix A).

This training document, outlining the design of tunnels used in combat hamlets and villages and discussing their uses, construction, specifications and maintenance, was captured by Korean troops on 24 September 1967 in South Vietnam. It details everything from the size of the entrances and their positions relative to each other to the numbers in digging teams and what they should do with the soil they pull out of the ground. It also reveals how important the tunnel systems were to the Vietcong, referring frequently to their troops being outgunned by the Allies.

Facing the odds they did, and knowing the ingenuity and industry of Vietnamese people, it's little wonder that they had made a science out of the tunnels' construction, location and operation. Reading that document, you begin to appreciate how well organised, well constructed and tactically important the Vietcong's tunnel systems were.

It's hard to comprehend how much material and information was gathered during Crimp. They had found a tunnel system that went down six levels and—they would later discover—stretched for almost 60 square kilometres (twice the area of the Australian Capital Territory). About 100 weapons, as well as ammunition, grenades, radios and gasmasks were retrieved. More than 100,000 pages of documents were recovered, plus food, medical equipment, eight bicycles, four typewriters and lists of both cadre members and assassination targets.

But the tunnels weren't completely destroyed, mainly because the Allies didn't fully understand their range or complexity, according to one Vietcong officer who was there at the time. Crimp drove the Vietcong out into surrounding villages for a while, forcing them to leave their equipment behind. But they came back at night to collect what they could and returned later to rebuild and restore their most potent weapon in the war.

Even so, Crimp was a huge success for the Allied troops and the Australians in particular. After 3 Field Troop's discoveries in Cu Chi, a general order was issued by General Williamson, the Allied Forces Commander in South Vietnam, to all Allied forces that tunnels had to be properly searched whenever they were discovered.

Thus the legend of the Tunnel Rats was born.

# 12. LIKE A ROLLING STONE

It was a very different 3 Field Troop that returned from Cu Chi; they'd lost a comrade and discovered the Vietcong's secret weapon. They had confronted death on a daily basis—either above ground in fire fights or below ground in airless tunnels—and they had come up trumps.

'I suppose we must all have been in some kind of shock when we returned to Bien Hoa from Crimp,' says Sandy MacGregor. 'We'd gone straight from one big operation to an even bigger one. We had virtually rewritten the rule book as far as engineer tasks in modern warfare went. And we'd lost a damn fine soldier.

'For the first time I saw unity of purpose in that boozing, brawling lot. OK, they weren't all bad, by any means. But there weren't many saints in 3 Field Troop either. As I've said many times, the sudden realisation that this war was real made the men stick by each other because they knew they needed their comrades to stick by them. Mateship was everything.'

The troop landed back at Bien Hoa on 14 January and one of Sandy's first tasks was to write a letter of sympathy to Bob's widow.

'They actually teach young officers how to do that at military college but it's a skill you hope you never have to use,' says Sandy. 'She would already have received the bad news, but a dead soldier's commanding officer often prefers to add his personal condolences.'

Sandy didn't have much time to enjoy the relative peace and comfort of camp before he was whisked off to Saigon for a press conference intended to tell the world about what they had found in the Vietcong tunnels. Before they met the journalists, he was quickly coached in how to handle questions from the 100 or more international reporters who had assembled there. Then it was into the fray, with Brigadier General Ellis Williamson, the commander of 173rd Airborne Brigade, and Colonel Alex Preece, the commanding officer of 1 RAR.

After a fairly orderly start to the session, when they outlined Operation Crimp, they went to questions and answers, which is when it got pretty hectic. Having been in the thick of it all, Sandy was the star attraction and found himself surrounded by a swarm of reporters and cameramen all firing questions at him and calling his name.

'I would be answering one question while listening to the next, then turning back to answer a supplementary from the first guy. It was pandemonium but I have to admit I enjoyed it,' he recalls. 'One reporter asked me how far I thought the tunnels system extended. I said about six miles. There was a gasp of surprise and maybe even disbelief. I wonder how they'd have reacted if I'd known the truth—that it was already more than 20 times that.'

But then, in a throwaway phrase, Sandy helped coin the name that would eventually be given to all the Allied troops who went down the Vietcong tunnels from that day on.

'An American journalist asked me what we called the guys who went down the tunnels and I said we called them tunnel ferrets,' he recalls. 'This bloke had never heard of ferrets so I explained that we sent ferrets down holes to chase out rabbits and rats. Another journo said, "Ah, tunnel rats" and that was it. The name stuck.

'Some American troops had gone down the tunnels after they saw Australians investigating them at Cu Chi but it was only following this press conference that General Westmoreland issued an edict that in future all tunnels had to be searched because of the huge amount of intelligence that could be gathered there.'

■ ■ ■ ■

The troop had three weeks of respite before they went on Operation Roundhouse on 4 February. They were to join a search-and-destroy mission about 15 kilometres north of Bien Hoa. It should have been straightforward but these things never are. Roundhouse, although it seemed a simple enough prospect on paper, turned out to have the highest number and greatest concentration of booby traps. And that in turn led to another tactical innovation from 3 Field Troop and a shift in how the army deployed engineers.

It's a basic principle of military engineering that dissipating your forces means weakening them. You keep your engineers together so as to use them most efficiently. Vietnam changed all that. But the sappers' job increasingly involved looking for, and dealing with, booby traps. Now, in jungle warfare, when a company is separated from another company it's very difficult to get engineers across from one to the other. You have to have a protection party. You go as a patrol and in scrub country you could take an hour to travel 500 metres.

Initially 3 Field Troop had all their men on battalion headquarters, waiting to respond to a report from the infantry that there was a booby trap or a tunnel or whatever, and they would go out to them. But they had the same problem going from battalion headquarters to each company as they had going from company to company. It could take an hour, and that's too long. If a booby trap goes up, you want instant action—one booby trap always meant there were more around.

So Sandy suggested putting four engineers in a demolition team and attaching one demolition team to each infantry company. They kept a reserve of a dozen or so men back with battalion HQ ready to go forward for major engineering tasks, and that worked a lot better. Now, a company has three platoons. So then they tried having two demolition teams of three men each so that one team could be with each of the two forward platoons. This worked better still.

By the end of our tour in Vietnam, they'd have mini-teams of two operating—that is, a team of two with each platoon—which would become the standard for engineers throughout the rest of the war and may even continue right up to the present day for jungle warfare.

'It's a principle of war that you concentrate your forces. As soon as you start penny-packeting, you run big risks,' says Warren Lennon, who became Sandy's commanding officer. 'And particularly in the case of engineers, and particularly when you're building, if you concentrate your forces and hold them together, you can usually achieve much more than the sum of the parts. That was an old principle of engineering warfare, that to break down to less than peak size would cease to be reliable.

'However, the nature of some combat tasks was such that the break up into mini-teams was appropriate. We could enjoy the luxury of tailor-made forces to do what had to be done. We would have many teams or small groups of engineers moving with the infantry and they'd be sufficient to give them immediate action support so that if they clipped a booby trap on the trail then someone was there to immediately attend to it. But if they encountered tunnels or caves or substantial fortifications, then they knew they wouldn't have the resources to handle it and would call on reinforcements, which could be sent by helicopter.'

An interesting side effect of this was that the engineers had to carry yet more weight on their backs than they were carrying already. There were basic bits of equipment that all the mini-teams needed, and as the overall load went from being divided between four men, to three men, to two men, the individual burden rose.

'My pack was always heavy and that's thanks to Les Colmer,' says Sandy MacGregor. 'Les was my batman for the first half of the tour, and part of his job was to pack and unpack my kit for me while I was attending to the running of the troop. I only found out long after we'd got home that Les and my radio operator would load any additional gear such as tins of rations and a spare radio battery into my pack, to lighten their own load. So much for the privileges of rank.'

'I can't deny it,' confirms Les. 'But he was much bigger and stronger than me.'

On the fifth day of Roundhouse—the operation was

extended by a few days while they were in the field—they found a huge cache of 1800 rice bags, which they set about extracting from the area. Sandy expected the cache to be heavily booby-trapped, but there were only a couple of grenades in among the bags. However, the tracks all around were laced with booby traps, one of which came very close to taking out Sandy, Billy Coolburra and Bob Billman.

'We were in the bush and the path ahead was booby-trapped. I said to Mr MacGregor, "There's booby traps down there",' recalls Billy Coolburra. 'He said he wanted to go another way but there were booby traps down there too. He told me to go ahead—we had to go through because we had to get to where we were going by a certain time. We would normally bypass something like that but we were in a hurry.

'Me and Bob Billman were the scouts on that particular operation. The Vietcong had set up the booby traps three ways—one you could see, another that was hidden but was false and a third hidden wire that was the real thing. Sure enough, we tripped off a tripwire and that booby trap fell down within inches of my face. I saw the pin come out and the striking pin go down and then the puff of smoke came out. It can only have happened in a fraction of a second, but it seemed to take a long time.

'I thought I was a goner, but the bomb never went off. That was the only time I ever back-answered Mr MacGregor. I told him he was silly making us go through there—he should have had more sense. He was OK. He said we had a job to do and we just had to do it.'

Sandy recalls it vividly and knows exactly what Billy meant about it seeming to happen in slow motion: 'I remember hearing the click and thinking "Here we go!" I couldn't fault Billy for losing his temper at me. When you've just about had your head blown off, you're entitled to speak your mind.'

Apart from the booby traps, the operation was uneventful, with the destruction of grenades, artillery shells and two 6-metre bridges keeping the engineers out of mischief. But on 19 February, ten days after they returned from Roundhouse, they went on another big operation which again saw them having to change their tactics to suit the circumstances.

Operation Rolling Stone took them to an area about 10 kilometres to the east of Ben Cat, which was 20 kilometres north-west of Bien Hoa. They went as engineer support for 1 RAR, which was providing infantry cover for the American 1 Engineer Battalion, who were building a large road in the area. Although there wasn't much for 3 Field Troop to do as engineers, they were impressed, watching the Americans build this beautiful big 15-metre-wide road at a rate of more than a kilometre a day.

To begin with, there were a lot of village searches and some booby-trap work. And the dispersal of the sappers into smaller units continued. Having gone down to two teams of three per company, this was when they experimented with three mini-teams of two, a pattern that would remain until the end of their tour and beyond. But local Vietcong forces were harassing the construction workers and booby-trapping the construction sites and gravel pits at night, so the Aussies of 1 RAR were soon involved in night-time patrols against them.

For the first time the Vietcong were up against an enemy who could move silently through the jungle just as well as they could. And one company was so short-handed that they formed the sappers attached to them—two per platoon, plus the sapper corporal on company HQ—into another infantry section of seven men to help with the patrols. The sappers acquitted themselves well and were highly praised by both the platoon and company commanders.

All the Vietcong activity around the Rolling Stone site pointed to one thing: they were planning a major attack. At 10 pm on day 5, Major Ian McFarlane called for an artillery strike on an area where he could see lights shining, only 250 metres from 1 RAR's lines. His request was turned down. Those lights turned out to have been the assembly points for the three North Vietnamese battalions that had been force-marched 25 kilometres through jungle to attack the US engineers.

The attack was launched at midnight. About 2000 North Vietnamese regular soldiers attacked brigade headquarters, which they assumed would be a soft target. They were wrong. Suspecting something was up, the Americans had ranged an astonishing array of fire-power where they expected the attack to hit. The North Vietnamese, who had obviously had no time for a late reconnaissance, walked straight into their guns.

They did have some success, however, cheekily positioning mortars between 1 RAR and a US battalion and firing on both. The accusations about 'friendly fire' flew thick and fast until the mortar sites were discovered the next day. The attack cost the North Vietnamese dearly. Having been exhausted by their march to the battle, they were then cut to ribbons by the American guns then pounded by US and New Zealand artillery as they retreated.

More than 280 enemy dead were found the next day, with the loss of 11 US troops. The engineers were called on to oversee the burial of the Vietcong dead in a mass grave—a B-52 bomb crater that had been extended by bulldozers, then filled in. It's worth noting that one of the reasons the Vietnamese people today have a level of respect for Australians and New Zealanders (which Americans and Koreans perhaps don't enjoy) is that the Anzacs buried their enemy dead.

Three Field Troop's positions weren't actually attacked, apart from the mortars, but the North Vietnamese got very close. And the lengths they were prepared to go to engage Allied soldiers were worth bearing in mind for the future.

'Six months later, when we were sitting on the fringes of the Australian positions at Nui Dat, waiting for the Vietcong to come through our lines on their way to attack battalion HQ, I recalled the night 2000 of them marched 25 kilometres on a suicide mission,' says Sandy. 'I knew we couldn't be lucky all the time.'

# 13. THE LAST DETAIL

Three Field Troop's second-in-command, Lieutenant Geoff Stewart, was long overdue to lead the men on his own and Sandy MacGregor was spending a lot of time at MAC-V (Military Assistance Command, Vietnam) briefing other officers on what they'd found in Cu Chi, so Geoff took the reins for Operation Silver City.

Silver City took 41 members of the troop 25 kilometres north of Bien Hoa for a total of 14 days. The troop was to provide basic engineer support for 1 RAR, which in turn was backing an assault by the American 173rd Airborne Brigade on a suspected Vietcong headquarters complex to the north and west of a sharp dogleg in the Song Be.

The Allies' experience in Rolling Stone—that Australian

jungle patrols could keep Vietcong activity to a minimum—meant that 1 RAR soon found themselves in a jungle war with the Vietcong. And the sappers were again called upon to augment their engineering skills with some basic infantry work.

One of Brian Hay's most vivid memories of the Vietnam War was of being among those to leave Bien Hoa in the initial wave of helicopters heading to Silver City: 'I remember the very first time I went in on the very first stick of the first chalk [group]. I recall that we left Bien Hoa and we gathered height and it was quite exciting to look back and see the sky filled with choppers as far back as the eye could see. Absolutely incredible. And then to look down on this mosaic, this patchwork of paddies and different other things, was just absolutely fantastic.

'All the doors were open and the guys were sitting on the edge—and nobody was strapped in. Something caught my eye and I could see these little flashes and little tiny bits of smoke away in the distance, down low on the right. And I can remember seeing a bit of action going on and I'm watching for a while, I could see jets going in and they were bombing and rocketing, they were beating the shit out of this place. And I gave the bloke next to me a nudge and I said, there's some poor bastard in trouble down there. I pointed and he looked and we watched. We could see the action coming towards you then drifting away on the right.

'As we started to go past it, as it started to recede, we saw our gunships peel off and go in too. They started to beat the shit out of the area as well. We said, geez, shit, some poor sod is in trouble down there. And then we started to lose height and then it dawned on me that this is where we were bloody going. Anyway, we came down over the Song Be River and did a complete 180 degrees, back over the river and then onto a big open patch of ground that ran parallel to the Song Be. As we came down over the river all the door-gunners opened up on command—and remember, all rounds of ammunition fired from the air is a tracer. And you could see all this tracer and where it goes to, hitting the ground and bouncing away. We got lower and lower and eventually ceased firing and the chopper hit the ground.

'We'd been taught that on a first wave attack, what you do is you jump off, lie on the ground, adopt a defensive position and wait for the choppers to leave. Nobody had bothered to tell our RSM. "Pig's arse!" he shouted. "Run! Get out! Run!" We didn't know if there was any sod out there after us or what. As we ran, the next stick hit the ground, three men ran from each side of the helicopter into the bush; the next stick hit the ground and they ran. Holy shit! It was action. The reason they fired so heavily into the area before landing was because the Vietcong were there and they knew we were coming because the choppers had landed there so many times before. I learned from that just how much I wanted to live.'

In this 'hot insertion', the idea was that most of the Vietcong would be driven off by the aerial pasting the helicopters and jets handed out. Before they left, the Allied troops encountered many small Vietcong units and at least one North Vietnamese regiment. Three Field Troop found themselves waterborne for the first time in Vietnam as they crossed the Song Be in search of rice caches.

'This was the last big operation for 1 RAR before the group withdrew from Bien Hoa and Vietnam,' says Geoff Stewart. 'Although of course the troop stayed on and went down to Vung Tau to prepare for 1 Task Force coming in. The aim of Silver City was to move into an area where it was known the Vietcong were operating. There were large rice caches in the area. Our work wasn't just with 1 RAR. We were also supporting a couple of companies from 1/503rd Battalion, which belonged to 173rd Airborne.

'We had the mini-teams operating at that stage, plus of course the group at battalion headquarters, which could move out to any of the larger finds such as the rice caches. Our particular role was to make sure the booby traps were neutralised and to destroy the rice. When we started the operation, the rice was being choppered back to Bien Hoa then being distributed through the ARVN network to the Vietnamese people. But on the third day of clearing rice and salt caches, a helicopter came in and was hit whilst landing on the very tight jungle pad that we had cut earlier that day.

All our noise must have attracted Vietcong attention. It was fairly obvious that the Vietcong were trying to capture the chopper and it was only artillery fire that drove them off.'

According to Dennis Ayoub, that was the second time the troop had been fired on at that rice cache.

'We knew they [the Vietcong] were there,' says Dennis. 'The first time was when "Tuggy" Tugwell was clearing the top of a salt and rice cache using a mine detector. We had ghosted around the cache and cleaned all the booby traps from ground level upwards. It was a particularly well-defended cache, with an intricate network of trip-wires. As soon as the shooting started, we hit the ground and got ready to help our infantry protection who were already returning fire. Tuggy was still on top of the rice and I saw him lift his earpiece to get a better idea of the sound he thought he was hearing from his mine detector. In fact, what he was hearing was the sound of machine-gun fire.

'He was on top of six bags of rice that were already on a platform 2 feet off the ground, so he made a good target. It didn't take him long to get down when he realised the sounds were shooting and most of it was aimed at him.'

From then on, all the rice was destroyed where it was found, either by blowing it up or sprinkling CS gas crystals through it.

It wasn't just choppers that were the target when Geoff and the lads tried getting the rice out to a safe landing area.

'The Americans had provided four mechanical mules—light self-propelled wagons—and we would load them with rice and cart it back to a helicopter pad that had been secured by Bravo Company down by the river,' recalls Geoff Stewart. 'Being plant operators and drivers, Doc Livingstone, Mick McGrath, John Peters and Dennis Ayoub all wanted to drive them.

'It was on one of those trips that my batman [Doc Livingstone] was hit with a DH-10 mine—similar to our Claymore mine—when we were bringing these mules back down the track. So that practice also ceased after that.' Brian Hay was there to witness it all: 'Everybody hit the deck and got up afterwards, except for Doc,' says Brian. 'He was lucky. The only thing that saved Doc was the fact that he was wearing the radio. He was sitting up on the rice bags and the radio and its webbing took most of the impact. He's still picking bits of radio out of his back today.'

After the mine went off, the troop was under fire from Vietcong hidden in the surrounding jungle until infantry drove them off.

'When the mine went off, it knocked the mule over but the rice bags acted as protection,' says Geoff Stewart, who had been driving one of the mules. 'There were three other mules and the blokes just dropped down behind them and returned fire. The fire was coming from down the track on our left-hand side—the direction we'd been heading—and the platoon that had been protecting us all day were heading back to camp as this was the last trip of the day. But they were only about two to five minutes behind us, moving back down the track. So they came back down the track as soon as they heard the firing. And the enemy moved out. A couple of those Vietcong were killed when they accidentally ran into another platoon further away.'

According to Dennis Ayoub, Doc Livingstone had a premonition that they were going to be hit, but it was more based on logic and experience than any sixth sense.

'We broke all the rules,' says Dennis. 'We went in to a location three times without securing the location and without proper protection. We had an infantry section that looked after eight engineers who were doing the work, so it was a one-to-one ratio instead of a three- or even five-to-one ratio like it should have been. There was a contact further out on the second day, then closer to the rice caches on the third day. Later on we walked into the ambush. Doc Livingstone was badly knocked about, Johnny Peters got hit in the leg and one of the infantry guys was hit. I drove through that ambush. I was going too fast and these were assault troops that hit us. They showed good control. They let me through then hit the slower-moving vehicles behind me. There were four of us and they hit the middle one of the three behind me.

'The explosions had occurred and I was about 30 metres

away. I stopped the mule and I and the two guys that were with me ran back to the way we thought they were coming. When we got back to the site there was chaos. The blast had blown the middle mule over and there were ruptured bags everywhere. There were blokes moaning and groaning and leaves falling down everywhere and smoke and dust and all the things that you'd expect in a contact.'

Mick McGrath was there too. 'I was carrying the M-60 and I'd been riding mules out along that track, sitting on top of the rice and the salt caches,' recalls Mick. 'I'd done probably six or eight trips. It was going to be the last trip of the day and everybody was coming back in before dark and I said to Doc, "You've been on the mine detector all day; you take the radio back and I'll get it off you back at the river. I'll carry the mine detector back in for you." Because, you know, he was a pretty fair lump of a bloke even then, and it was pretty hot. He wasn't a bad bloke because we'd hutchied together several times, even though we were in different sections.

'So off he went down the road and he'd only gone about 300 metres from where we were doing this rice cache and up it went. Well, it could quite easily have been me sitting on it and it would have killed me, because Doc was such a heavily set bloke, and the radio had helped to absorb the shock, so what hit him would have gone straight through me and I'd have just bled to death before they could have done anything. When I got to Doc his arm was mangled and he was losing a lot of blood and Johnny Peters was sort of more in shock than anything else. He was obviously hurt but he was more in shock.

'One of the Americans that were driving the mules was a black guy. He had a bit of a wound to him but he was carrying on something stupid, screaming out "Lord, I'm coming to meet you", and all this. And this big American sergeant—he was a coloured bloke too—walked up and slapped him across the face said "Shut up, boy, you ain't nothing hurt as bad as what you will be if you don't shut up."'

At the time it looked as if Doc wasn't going to make it home. But he did. 'Doc was very badly hit and was evacuated,' says Geoff Stewart. 'In fact, we had to bring him back on one of the mules to the pad that was used for the rice near Bravo Company.'

The next day Bill Unmeopa and Tex Cotter were blown up—with no lasting damage—when they were delousing rice bags and one of the hidden grenades went off. 'That happened quite often,' says Geoff. 'And the only thing was that a lot of rice got spread around.'

At the end of Silver City, Geoff and Dennis Ayoub stayed behind to deal with a 1000-pound aerial bomb that had been dropped near the river but hadn't exploded.

'Colonel Preece had told me to blow it up on our withdrawal,' says Geoff. 'Of course, we couldn't blow it till all our troops and the choppers had gone, so the last chopper went some distance away from us while we set the fuses on it—we had to dig down beside it to set the charges. Then we high-tailed it across to the chopper and made off before it went up. The bomb made a fair racket when it went up.'

This wasn't the first time Geoff Stewart had come a bit close. Back at the end of Operation New Life, he was helping to transport a bulldozer back to Bien Hoa, as part of an American convoy, when one of the transporter's bogies snapped.

'The American commander wanted to blow the dozer up and leave it. But being an Aussie I said we couldn't afford to do things like that, so I brought that dozer back down while the rest of the convoy kept going,' says Geoff. 'In fact I drove that dozer while Doc Livingstone drove our Land Rover with a machine gun on the back. We brought it home after dark and we came under fire then. The dozers did five-and-a-half miles an hour flat-out in reverse, so it was a long trip. We were very lucky to get it back in because we literally walked it back to camp.' It was a productive trip—Geoff Stewart found the Willys jeep on the same operation.

Silver City was the last big operation 3 Field Troop undertook with 1 RAR, although the work they did at Vung Tau and the initial work at Nui Dat was done when they were still known as 3 Field Troop. Within weeks the task force would be arriving from Australia and they'd lose 'field' from their title as they were absorbed into the main body of engineers. For the first time they'd be fighting alongside national servicemen, and for the first time in Vietnam Sandy MacGregor would have an engineer as his commanding officer.

The last 3 Field Troop operation, Abilene, could hardly have been smaller. Corporal Ross Thorburn led four sappers who went along with 1 RAR into Phuoc Tuy province where they hoped to find and destroy two North Vietnamese regiments. As Ross reported, there wasn't much there for engineers to do. But they learned a lot about infantry work and on one occasion a sapper was used as forward scout to lead an American company into its cordon position at night.

The reason they could only spare five men for Abilene was because it started on 30 March. On 31 March the majority of the troop moved from Bien Hoa to Vung Tau to prepare it for the arrival of the Australian task force, while the remainder had the unenviable task of pulling down their base camp at Bien Hoa and salvaging as much as possible. It wasn't the end of their adventures—far from it—but it was definitely the end of an era.

# 14. PLAYING HARD

The men of 3 Field Troop had begun to see Bien Hoa as home. They were well set up and it was a good place to be after the stress of operating in the jungle. But while their discipline and commitment had been proved without question in the field, back at base things were different. However, there was a real comradeship building up between them that worked both on and off duty. The men worked in pairs, in a buddy system which would prove invaluable later in the war when new troops had to be trained to replace them. These friendships were sometimes forged under fire, sometimes over a couple of beers at night.

Sparrow Christie teamed up with Peter Ash as early as the voyage over: 'Peter and I, we were doing unarmed combat on the flight deck of the *Sydney* and had our bayonets out like a knife attack. You were supposed to go "HA!!" and the other guy would go "HA!!" and you're supposed to disarm them. We were only going through the motions and the instructor had a go at us and said put effort into it, so I had the bayonet this time and I went "HA!" a bit louder, so Peter went "HA!!" really loud and I pretended to be scared and threw my bayonet over the side.

'When it came to getting a new bayonet—which could have cost me five quid—I said we'd been putting our heart and soul into the unarmed combat. I got a new bayonet but I never got charged for it. When we got to Vietnam I partnered Peter on all my operations. And you'd never get two blokes more different. You know Peter was a massive big bloke, whereas I was sort of small and insignificant. I carried the explosives, the weight, and Peter carried the detonators. But we always hutchied up together. It was just sort of unthinkable that I'd go out in the bush with anyone else other than Peter.

'We got on real well. I used to get cold when it was wet and I'd cuddle up to him in the bush. You've got to survive. We totally relied on each other. I felt completely safe with him and I'm sure he felt the same way. There was no way in the world would I have let him down. The infantry used to laugh at us because we used to argue over whose turn it was to go down into bunkers and tunnels first. They thought we were mad for going in at all.'

Mick McGrath teamed up with Doc Livingstone early in the piece too. It was a relationship which endured possibly because of its strange beginning out on an operation.

'Doc and I had to hutchie up together and we always looked for a couple of trees to tie the tent to,' recalls Mick. 'So I got the bush knife out and I started cutting branches and all of a sudden there's this slithery looking green object in front of me, so I lopped its head off. Anyway, the head landed near Doc and he said "Jesus Christ, what are you doing to me?" Then he looked and saw what it was and he said, "Shit a brick" and that was just the start of it. Before we'd even bedded down for the night we had snakes among us.

'Anyway, the artillery was firing from positions next to us so you can imagine how much rest we got that night. And the next morning I'm out early to go to the listening post and there was a bit of rain about so I took my groundsheet with me. When I got there it was pouring down so I pulled the groundsheet over me with the barrel of my rifle underneath there too. Eventually, when the rain stopped and I just shrugged the groundsheet off and I don't know, for some reason I looked down and there was the biggest scorpion you've ever seen in your life. He'd crawled under the groundsheet with me to keep dry.'

Snow Wilson remembers well two occasions on which he was sharing shelter—in the form of an American poncho—with his 'twin' Billy Coolburra, the first being when they were out looking for a little female company. 'We were in a very interesting palace of love, I guess you could call it. Two delightful young ladies had attracted our eye and the ceiling of it was an American Army issue poncho. I'll never forget it and it was pouring rain and there was a huge rip down the middle of it and he's on one side and I'm on the other side. The next time a poncho of that order comes to mind we were in the Mekong Delta. I was on machine-gun picket and young William had just gone back to bed and a mongoose crawled over his arm and he couldn't work out what it was. He was asleep and he thought it was his girlfriend, then he decided it was a snake and then he didn't know what it bloody was, but it was furry so he went for the machete and got stuck into it.

'But the only thing he did was ripped his half of our hutchie to ribbons so when it started raining about three hours later he crawled into my side. It created a bit of an argument until I pushed the black bastard back into his side.'

But it wasn't all brotherly love. Bullies would lean on whoever would let them and there would still be fights, although more often than not others would step in to separate the combatants.

'There was always a few knuckle-ups but I don't reckon we had near as many as what the battalions did,' says Mick McGrath. 'I've seen guys in the battalions, you know, they'd have a fight and everybody would stop and watch the fight to make sure that nobody fought dirty. As soon as the fight was over they'd shake hands and go back as if nothing had happened. But in the early days the fighting and the bickering that went on in our mob wasn't just a fistfight and finish, it almost ended up like gang war.'

Sparrow Christie recalls one memorable fight which was halted at gunpoint: 'I saw one stoush going on outside our tent and Brian Ticknell—he was our lance corporal—came out with his Owen gun. He threatened to shoot them all up if they didn't stop. So I raced inside and got my rifle and backed him up. But Ticknell was the one that got in the shit, not me; everybody seemed to forget that I was there too.'

More by accident than design, it seemed each operation while they'd been in Bien Hoa had been more difficult than the previous one. The pressures were growing and that meant the guys had to find ways of letting off steam. Most of it was comparatively innocent fun—and it was better than having them beating each other up—but one day, to Sandy MacGregor's horror, the 173rd Airborne complained that someone had stolen their flag. Now, losing your flag is about as shameful a thing as can happen to soldiers and the Americans were beside themselves with rage and embarrassment. For some reason, they decided that 3 Field Troop were behind the outrage and they wanted the culprits caught and handed over.

'I was furious. How dare they suggest that my men would do such a thing?' recalls Sandy. 'We were too busy to play schoolboy pranks and too respectful of our allies to commit such a dishonourable act. I clung to that belief for more than 20 years, and it was only when the missing American flag turned up at a 3 Field Troop reunion in Sydney a couple of years ago that I finally conceded that my blokes did it.'

Sandy MacGregor tried to keep discipline pretty tight, but he couldn't afford to have men locked up when they should have been out on operations. So he devised a punishment detail of digging a swimming pool and anybody who crossed the line would find themselves filling sandbags for a few days. Typically, the sappers turned the punishment into a pleasure: the swimming pool was on the way back from the canteen and the blokes would always have somebody prepared to drop in a couple of cans to make sure they weren't thirsty.

'I think I got more to drink in the swimming pool than in the canteen,' says Billy Coolburra. 'I'd put a shovelful of sand into a sandbag and then hand the shovel to Snow, or whoever I was with, and he'd hand me the can of beer. Then, when he was shovelling, I would drink, then vice versa. That swimming pool never did get finished.'

Sandy was very strict about not drinking on duty, but some of the guys always found some way round it, most notably Waxy Rayner. Sandy often suspected him of being drunk and was always surprised that it would only take a couple of cans at night to see him three sheets to the wind. It was Dennis Ayoub who discovered his little secret.

'Waxy was the RAEME mechanic who used to keep the

old Buddha engine going. Waxy, who was about 42 and had been in World War II, had purloined some sort of travel box, the type used for theodolites, which had been lined with felt on the inside. The old bastard had buried this in the area between the wheel tracks of the parking place for the road grader. Given his job, no one would ever suspect him for being under the grader at any time. But he had welded a tap on to the hidden box so he could run booze from it over ice.

'One day, when I was parking the grader, I saw the ground move, since I had not lined the grader up correctly. I dug down and knocked the top off the box and there was all this cold piss. From that day on, I always had a good supply of booze.'

Dennis was also there when Frankie Mallard decided to souvenir an unexploded aircraft cannon round he'd found on a patrol: 'When the planes were doing a strafing run, they might be reloading or recocking their weapons and a round would come out. We weren't supposed to touch them but Mallard decided he'd take this one home and turn it into a bookend or something. Anyway, he had the round in the vice on the workshop bench and there he is cutting away at it with a hacksaw.

'I don't know if you've ever cut metal with a hacksaw but it gets bloody hot after a while,' says Dennis. 'There was Mallard sawing away and the thing went off. It blew lots of little holes in Mallard's clothes and a few little holes in Mallard and Craftsman Carl Richards, both of whom had to go to the RAP for attention. It stuffed the vice and the hacksaw. How he didn't lose his hands I'll never know.'

Meggsie Dennis nearly wiped out a tentful of guys when he decided to empty his Owen gun by sliding the firing mechanism back and forth, rather than taking the magazine off and emptying it by hand.

'We were bludging—we were supposed to be working—and Laurie [Hodge, Staff Sergeant] used to listen to make sure the tractor was working,' recalls Dennis Ayoub. 'But we used to leave the throttle tied back on the tractor then go inside the tent and play cards. Meggsie was just back from a small operation and he had to empty his gun. He had two options: he could either take all the bullets out of his gun or he could take them round to the creek at the back of our place and fire them all off, in which case you had to clean your weapon.

'Meggsie, me, Mick McGrath and Alan Brown were in the tent, even though Brownie didn't live in it. The Owen gun has a fixed firing pin and Meggsie had covered it with his thumb and was letting the bullets just slide out. Then one of them went off and before he could take his finger off the trigger, he had fired all his bullets into the other side of the tent.'

Nobody was hurt, but it was a near thing, as Mick Lee explains: 'I was up the gun tower at the time and I heard the shots and I looked at the tent and see Alan come out white as a ghost and I thought someone had been shot. But later on I found out that just prior to Meggsie's gun going off, Brownie had sat up on the bed. The bullets went through this old wooden box we used to use to put our clothes in, through the pillow where his head was, then up the tent walls and then it finished up through the roof and that's why Alan walked out white as a ghost.

'It was funny later on—well, actually, two weeks later I had some green singlets and things folded up in the make-shift wardrobe. I shook them and a bloody round fell out. After that I said to Meggsie, "You know where you're sleeping from now on, don't you?" He got over to my corner 'cause all the rain used to come in through the holes.'

There was another moment of danger one night for some of the American visitors to 3 Field Troop's casino, as Geoff Stewart relates: '101 Air Cav was one of the units near us. One night after several drinks they were going out of our wire and heading for their own when they saw six or seven people wandering along. "Hullo!" they said. "What are you guys doing?" The only trouble was that the other guys were in black pyjamas—the Vietcong were inside the base perimeter. I don't know who got the biggest fright, but both lots ran off in opposite directions as fast as their legs would take them. The next morning the guys were grey when they realised what had happened.'

Sandy MacGregor was not immune from the pranksters.

Les Colmer, his batman, used to make him carry extra rations, which Les would then eat. And Sandy could never understand why he only ever got ham and lima beans in his ration packs until Les explained years later that anybody who was passing used to swap Sandy's ration pack for theirs if he had something more interesting.

'On reflection, I wouldn't have eaten anything hot, or ever had a hot cup of tea or coffee at all, if it hadn't been for what Les Colmer prepared for me,' says Sandy. 'I simply didn't have time to do that, let alone to check and pack my rations. I guess it was easier just to carry it all. As to what I ate, I didn't know, it was invariably after dark.'

Les was doing his best to look after Sandy, within reason, but when push came to shove it was every man for himself.

'On Operation Rolling Stone we were working on the road and the ground was that thick and hard,' says Les. 'So off Sandy goes to the orders group and tells me to dig a weapons pit, get the tucker ready and put up the hutchie. But the ground was too hard to dig much more than a scrape, which was OK until they started shooting at us in the middle of the night. I was out of the hutchie first and into the hole. He wanted me to get out of the bottom but I said no friggin' way. So he said "I'm the Captain . . . I get in first." I said, "I dug the friggin' hole and I'm staying." I was supposed to dig two holes but it was so hard I only managed one. I don't think he forgave me for it for a while; he was a bit grumpy for a few days.'

Like most enlisted men, Snow Wilson loved making fun of authority. He started visiting the officers' club on the air base after he'd been bounced by an American Provo while wearing civvies. 'The next time I went down I put a little Royal Australian Engineers bar on my shoulder. They must have thought I was a WO. Their warrant officers had a gold bar that was split in three, there was gold and then brown and then gold, depending on the classification of warrant officer. In I went and I reckon I got away with that for about four weeks. I can tell you, their women were better looking.'

Les Colmer had a delusion of grandeur at Bien Hoa when he was waiting for Laurie Hodge, who was supposed to be picking up some movies for the camp cinema.

'I got bored hanging around so I put a piece of wire on the mudguard of the Land Rover and screwed it in. Then I bought one of them little flags and stuck it on, which basically made whoever was in the car a general,' says Les. 'So when we come back and go through the gate the Yanks are going crazy at the checkpoints, all running out saluting.

'Laurie was sitting beside me in the front and said, "What do we do?" and I said, "Salute 'em." By the time we got back to camp, Sandy was on the phone saying, "Tell Colmer to get rid of that bloody flag", and he didn't even know it was me. That's what you call an educated guess.'

With the move on to Vung Tau, and the incorporation into the larger force, the fun and games had to stop. Or at least be pulled back a bit. As the men of 3 Field Troop would soon discover, the adjustment to life at Vung Tau clearly wasn't going to be as simple as relocating their tents and equipment.

# 15. ON THE BEACH

To some of the men of 3 Field Troop, leaving Bien Hoa was as great a wrench as leaving Australia. It had become their home those past six months or so and they had worked hard to make it a little more than merely habitable. On the other hand, they were excited. Vung Tau was a change of direction as well as a change of scenery. Vung Tau itself was one of the main holiday destinations for Saigon when the country was still under French rule. Vietnam's towns were once elegant outposts of French colonialism, blending East and West in a fashion reminiscent of Singapore and Shanghai before the Second World War.

But in the northern spring of 1966, the bars were full of prostitutes and their American, Aussie and Kiwi clientele. The beaches were polluted and the signs of war were everywhere. It was also the place where the men of 3 Field Troop had first set foot on Vietnamese soil and few of them were happy to be back there.

'I'd forgotten that we'd even landed in Vung Tau,' says Keith Kermode. 'We were going to this place that we had just breezed through. I think, looking back, that we were resentful because we'd built this camp in Bien Hoa, we were moving away from the Americans and it was another change. On the other hand, the Australians were going to form their own unit. There were other battalions coming over and I suppose that offset the disappointment.

'But after all the hard work we'd done building Bien Hoa it was bloody terrible. We lived like dogs in the early days in Vung Tau, living on sand dunes. We'd had a few home comforts in Bien Hoa and then we lob on these bloody sand dunes and all the work starts again. And after a couple of months this task force arrived and all our ill-gotten gains were pilfered from us. We were quite resentful.'

Geoff Stewart and a handful of men were left to dismantle and transport what couldn't be taken with the main body of the troop, while the bulk of the men headed to Vung Tau. Their job was to build a base camp for the Aussies of 5 RAR and 6 RAR, and the Australian Logistic Support Group (ALSG). When that was complete, they were to head up to Nui Dat in the jungle, to create the Australian Task Force (ATF) operational base.

Just getting to Vung Tau was a major operation: 'Our dozers and graders and four operators—namely Geoff Guest, Dennis Ayoub, Johnny Peters and myself—were the last to be loaded and airlifted to Vungers, but due to lack of aircraft we were stranded at Bien Hoa Air Base for four days waiting for C-130 Hercs,' says Bernie Pollard. 'Needless to say, the four of us played up pretty hard during that time, especially in Bien Hoa and the base PX [the supply store]. At 6 am on the fifth morning, the American loadmaster dug us out (more than a little hungover) from under our machines with word that four Hercs were ready to be loaded. Beau Guest (being sober) loaded the first TD-15B, followed by myself.

'Everything was going fine as I backed the dozer up the plane's ramp,' says Bernie, 'but just as the TD-15B was on the point of balance at the top of the ramp, I had this horrible sensation that the plane was coming down on top of me, what with the diesel fumes pumping into the interior of the plane, combined with a "mild" hangover. I decided it was time to vacate. I shut off the engine, locked the brakes and bailed out onto the tarmac, dry-retching all the way.

'The sergeant loadmaster was screaming: "Get that goddam tractor off ma plane." Looking around, I saw that the Herc had reared up with the nose-wheel a good ten feet off the ground. Dennis, Guesty and Johnny Peters were standing back killing themselves laughing—I was feeling decidedly off colour! The loadmaster had forgotten to close the valves on the hydraulic rams that operate the plane's ramp, allowing the rams to start closing up under the weight of the dozer as it climbed higher into the aircraft.

'Dennis pointed out to the loadmaster that it would cause a lot of damage to the nose-wheel if we shifted the dozer, so after some debate, the loadmaster went off and rounded up about 30 men and had them all pack up into the cockpit and the front of the plane, which managed to bring the nose of the plane back down enough for me to finish loading the dozer.'

Although the troop wouldn't be going out on patrol to search tunnels and defuse booby traps, this was a new challenge, and much more like traditional engineer work: the first half of 'Facimus et Frangimus'—'We make and we break'. They were going to be building a huge camp from scratch and that was a huge challenge. The place where the army planned to build the camp was about 4 or 5 kilometres along the beach towards the mountains, which were occupied by Vietcong. In fact, the Vietcong used to walk along the beach into the town, which they used as a rest and recreation centre, as did the Aussies.

The first thing Sandy MacGregor did was to defy his orders that the camp should be built halfway to the mountains, because he wanted to be as close to the town as possible to have the support of the troops encamped there.

'I said, "Look, we've got limited engineers to prepare this

whole area in only two or three weeks, and there's no way in the world I'm going to work up there without our guys having some security. We should have infantry protection,"' he explains. 'We could have protected ourselves but it would have meant that we'd have no force to work with. We wouldn't have completed the job on time if half the blokes were guarding the other half.'

As it turned out, the brigadier agreed with Sandy and they moved back to right on the edge of the town, where they had all the support they needed. The next challenge they faced was purely an engineering one. They had to find a source of drinking water for the 2000 men who'd be passing through Vung Tau at any one time. Unlike the Americans, the Aussies—at the insistence of the army's chief medical officer—bathed in chlorinated water as well as drinking it and using it for cooking. This meant they used as much chlorinated water as all the American troops put together.

For two or three weeks they worked on getting water, and Sandy was racking his brains. They had two battalions and their supporting elements landing within a couple of weeks, at least 3000 people, so they needed a whole lot of water and the ability to clean and chlorinate it in huge amounts. They dug wells to get to the water under the sand, but they'd suck it all out in ten minutes. Then they discovered that in one spot in the strip of sand that they were on—between the town and the sea—there was water only a metre below the surface. And it was fresh water, not salt water, even though the sea was only 200 metres away. So they got their three dozers working flat-out in tandem in a continuous operation throughout one day, scraping a huge hole without stopping, which was the only way to keep the water level down. The dozers had to work flat-out to stay ahead of the water all the time, even though they pumped it out from a 'sump'. Eventually, they got down about 1.5 metres across an area about 20 metres by 30 metres when the water level got too high for the dozers (this was a good sign, of course). Then they deepened it by using a drag line and the water just poured into it. It was a huge pond and it was like having 400 wells all in the one area.

Then they flattened out the sand that they'd dug out and built up one end to create settling ponds where they chlorinated the water and stored it in two giant 10,000-gallon pillow tanks—so called because they looked like huge black rubber pillows—that Geoff Stewart had ferreted out. In fact, the pillow tanks were designated as petrol storage equipment, but they nabbed four of them because they knew they'd have to repeat the process at Nui Dat, the new operational base for the Australian task force.

So, against all the odds, they had a fantastic water system ready by the time the main body of troops arrived.

'Typically, I ended up being hauled over the coals,' says Sandy MacGregor. 'Some major complained I had taken the petrol equipment—the pillow tanks and the pumps which were earmarked for the Australian Transport Corps yet to arrive in Vung Tau. So I asked how else I was supposed to establish a water point. "Find another way," he said. "No," I said, "you bloody well find another way—we haven't been allocated any equipment to do the job." I was damned proud of that water point and I still am.'

Call it karma or coincidence but the whole operation almost ground to a halt when the the troop was sent a batch of contaminated diesel which had obviously been drained from the bottom of a tank somewhere and was full of dirt and rust. Murphy's Law being what it is, they only discovered it after all their tractors and dozers had been fuelled up then started breaking down halfway through their jobs.

'The fuel filters were clogged—normally you'd fit new ones after you'd cleaned out the fuel tanks,' said Dennis Ayoub. 'The trouble was that all our machines were Internationals, whereas the Americans, who were our immediate source of spare parts, only had spares for General Motors and Caterpillar engines. We had a lot of sand to move to prepare the ground for all the troops arriving. Without tractors, we weren't going to be very effective. Then Waxy Rayner had the bright idea of taking the tops off the fuel filters, pulling all the fibre and shit out and stuffing some sanitary towels into the space. It worked like a dream and we were sent into Vung Tau to buy up all the sanitary towels we could find and bring them back to camp.

'You don't think about the effects of these things at the time, and even if you did, the main priority was the war effort, so we bought up the lot and ended up with a tent full of boxes of the bloody things. Sure enough, it was only a matter of days before we realised that we'd created an artificial shortage of Modess or whatever they were. They were made overseas and they weren't the first thing they'd load on ships for Vietnam, so it was panic stations for the local girls.

'Of course, as soon as we realised this, whenever we had a night in town, we'd nip round the back of the supply tent, cut a slit in the back of a box and slide a couple of packets out. Some of the boxes were empty by the time they were opened,' he laughed. 'Anyway, with a couple of Modess packets you could get a girl for a whole night, 'cause they all knew they were going to need them at some stage. The funny thing is, at that time there was a clampdown on the black market in Yank cigarettes and PX discount whisky. But nobody ever cottoned on to the Aussies' black market in sanitary towels.'

Their larrikin spirit was irrepressible but Sandy was beginning to lose his autonomy as commander of a troop which had been very much left to its own devices. Now the Australian Army was making a much bigger commitment to Vietnam and there were more officers arriving every day—more 'arrogant young pricks' (to use Sandy's description)—who either didn't care that 3 Field Troop had spent six months blazing a trail for them, or took it as some sort of affront that he, a mere captain, had seen more action than they could dream of. All which spelled trouble for the whole troop.

First of all, the Army Logistical Support Group (ALSG) advance party decided that their position atop a hill was too good for mere sappers and they were told to move further down to much less hospitable ground. It may have had nothing to do with it, but a few days later a conference of officers on top of the same hill was brought to a halt when a person or persons unknown cut through the guy ropes on the marquee they were in and it collapsed on top of the meeting. Three Field Troop was blamed, but nothing could ever be proved. Even to this day, nobody has ever owned up.

Then some of the new officers who had arrived thought it was out of order that the sappers should have hot showers when they were forced to shower in cold water. They were told that the troop had paid for all the fittings themselves with their own money but they wouldn't listen. They decided they needed the showers more than the engineers did and commandeered them. Big mistake.

'Some colonel obviously hadn't done much man-management or leadership training,' explained Dave Cook. 'He decided he was going to keep our shower blocks that we'd worked very hard to get. He was always first in the shower but this particular morning his batman beat him in and bloody near shit himself. Wherever he looked there were little booby traps hooked up all over the bloody place with two or three ounces of Vietcong explosive.'

It looked like a good Vietcong job but the booby traps never went off because they were never intended to. The untrained eye couldn't tell that the charges weren't primed. The only people who could were the bomb disposal boys—that is, 3 Field Troop. Suffice it to say that in delousing the showers, removing the charges and checking that it was safe, which was carried out by 3 Field Troop, of course, the showers were rendered useless. The prime suspects were, of course, the Vietcong, closely followed by the sappers.

'I'm sure many of our superiors thought that the Vietcong and 3 Field Troop were one and the same,' says Sandy. 'I didn't know until recently that the culprit for this outrage was Davey Cook. He deserves a medal because he really expressed the troop's feeling at the time. I wasn't interested in finding the guilty party. No harm was done and justice was served.'

A few days after they had been moved off the top of the hill, the ALSG signallers decided they wanted the 'bench' the engineers had cleared and occupied halfway down a sand dune. A couple of nights after, there was a mysterious fire near one of the signaller's tents which burnt out their entire lines. Eventually the engineers were moved from prime spots so many times that Sandy MacGregor finally chose the lowest, hottest, noisiest and least promising area he could find.

They mightn't be as comfortable but at least they'd be left in peace to get on with doing their job.

Having tried to steal their showers and any spot they'd made habitable, ALSG turned their attentions to Buddha, which Geoff Stewart had brought from Bien Hoa. Buddha was the generator they'd recovered from Saigon, repaired, using their own money, and kept running with their skill and ingenuity. Typically, the logistical support guys decided they needed it more than the engineers did.

'I had planned to take it up to Nui Dat with us, where it could have powered the whole of 1 Field Squadron,' explains Sandy. 'But no, these ALSG wankers overruled me again. The blokes of 3 Field Troop were getting mightily tired of being messed around and I think they were blaming me for not standing up to my superiors. All I can say is that I had stood up to them once or twice too often as it was. I would argue with them but they just weren't listening.'

After the booby-trapping of the showers and the burning of the signallers' tents, there were no prizes for guessing what was going to happen next. Waxy Rayner, the RAEME engineer who had brought Buddha back to life and had kept it going all those months, went down with a big screwdriver and took the governor assembly off it, which meant the engine would just get faster and faster until it exploded. Dennis Ayoub remembers the night well.

'I knew something was going to happen but I'd broken

curfew and gone into Vung Tau,' recalls Dennis. 'On the way back I could hear old Buddha racing. I was a plant operator and I knew a bit about diesel engines. They normally only go at about 800 revs per minute, but tonight she was doing about 2000. I got down to where Buddha was and there were two-foot flames shooting out of the exhaust. I was pissed but I knew to keep clear. As my eyes adjusted to the light, I saw all these characters standing in the shadows watching. The ALSG blokes were running around like headless chooks. One of them came up to me and said "Turn it off—it's going to explode." I retorted that I knew it was going to explode—that's why I wasn't going anywhere bloody near it.'

Buddha did explode and a couple of the guys said they saw Waxy Rayner sitting up on a sandhill crying his eyes out as it melted down before them. All that work for nothing. The troop could have used Buddha when they got to Nui Dat but they had plenty to keep them occupied when they got there. And as for the ALSG blokes, they must have been glad to see them go. Fighting the Vietcong can't have seemed any harder than scrapping with 3 Field Troop.

When the troop first got to Nui Dat, about 40 kilometres north-east of Vung Tau, it was just a hill beside a road in the middle of rubber plantations. Within a month, it would be the military base for the entire Australian war effort in

Vietnam, with a battalion on the northern side, another on the eastern side alongside the armoured corps, then the engineers and artillery were down south.

For that to happen they had to build roads, establish water points and clear land for accommodation tents—all of the stuff they'd done in Vung Tau they had to do again. Except this time they didn't have close-in protection. The 5th Battalion of Australian infantry was out there somewhere, occupying the area, but the nearest company to the sappers would have been a good mile away and they never saw much of them. The Vietcong were very active in the area. The enemy operating in the area was the 274th and 275th Regiment, reinforced by D445 Battalion and a battalion of North Vietnamese regulars—they knew the Australian Army was coming and, if they couldn't prevent it, they wanted to slow progress down as much as possible. The 173rd Airborne Brigade had carried out a clearing operation to assist the occupation of Nui Dat a week before 5 RAR joined them. One of the American companies lost eight killed and 23 wounded in an ambush.

The sappers flew in helicopters with 5 RAR to occupy Nui Dat, and their trucks and equipment came by road. When they landed, 3 Field Troop was effectively operating as infantry, helping to protect HQ while looking after themselves. It was no mere exercise; the very first night there was enemy machine-gun fire at 5 RAR battalion HQ position.

'The enemy were firing uphill and some rounds went through Sapper Ian Biddolph's hutchie and his mess tins that were hanging inside,' recalls Dennis Ayoub. 'We had to put out clearing patrols, man guns and contend with some very nervous new diggers. Coming in from a patrol, Private Noack was the first national serviceman killed, on that same night.'

This was 3 Field Troop's most vulnerable period in the whole of their time in Vietnam. They had all their straightforward engineering work to do during the day, but day *and* night, they had only such protection as they could provide themselves—this went on for three weeks. It was the first time they'd had to put out patrols at night, with clearing patrols, night patrols and even standing patrols out there in the bush, ahead of their lines, as an early warning. They manned all their guns and were in a defensive position all the time and checked that their Claymore mines were set to fire at the enemy, in case the Vietcong had sneaked in and turned them around to be directed at the Aussies.

'Sometimes it was easy to forget we were engineers, because a lot of the time we just operated like infantry,' recalls Sandy. 'But every morning we'd be back at work, clearing and levelling and building and protecting. Battalion HQ claimed they were protecting us but I knew that we were terribly vulnerable. All eyes were on us. The Vietcong knew what we were doing—they knew the task force headquarters was being built. It was too big a job for them not to know what was going on. There would be about 8000 men there by the time we were fully set up and we had 21 days to get the basic infrastructure in place—6 RAR were to follow soon after 5 RAR.'

Nui Dat was 3 Field Troop's last home in Vietnam and Sandy was determined it would not be any of his men's last resting place. The move from Vung Tau to Nui Dat continued a major shift in Sandy's responsibilities. From being a lone wolf troop commander answerable to a variety of American and Australian superiors, but remote enough from them all to be able to run his own race, within a few weeks he would become a humble captain again, with a full hierarchy of engineer officers above him.

The troop's duties changed considerably too. They had new men to train and only a few weeks to teach them all they had learned in the nine months they had been in Vietnam. For the new guys it was a different kind of challenge. Three Field Troop was, by this time, a legend among Australian engineers. They had been there, done that. This ragtag band of serious soldiers and mischievous reprobates had become a battle-hardened band of anti-heroes.

'Everything the new boys had learned in Australia about the perils of Vietnam they had learned thanks to us,' Sandy says. 'We were their role models as soldiers and we'd won their respect, however grudgingly, before they ever set eyes on us. Our capacity for the pleasures of the flesh was legendary too. We were a hard act to follow.'

The lads in 3 Field Troop had three months to go. One RAR had gone home to be replaced by 5 and 6 Battalion and 1 Field Squadron had come in to provide engineer support under Warren Lennon. This was his first time in Vietnam and he was learning from 3 Field Troop, but he had concerns they might play the old soldiers and not knuckle down to the discipline of having a new boss.

'When I became the Squadron Commander of 1 Field Squadron in Vietnam, it included 3 Field Troop, which became 3 Troop,' recalls Warren Lennon. 'They, 3 Troop, had been working more or less independently and had earned themselves a big reputation. In that time they'd established some combat procedures that were new, when dealing with the particular problems they'd encountered, such as tunnels, with platoons within battalions. They were independent. And because of that, they were operating in many ways in a much stronger capacity than you'd normally expect from a troop. And, of course, Sandy was accepting much more responsibility—and I think strain—than you'd normally put on a troop commander.

'When I got there, I was looking forward to the opportunity to absorb them and provide a more substantial engineer force to back up what was obviously a much larger host unit to be supported. I'd had good relationships with both the officers with 3 Field Troop prior to their departure, so I was looking forward to having them as part of the squadron. I guess I was conscious that there might be some difficulties with the new boys arriving and trying to take over but I didn't perceive any of that happening. I was happy to listen to Sandy and what he'd done and we were more than happy to learn.

'Right at the outset 3 Field Troop had very much a sponsoring and teaching role, particularly the officers and NCOs, that helped the rest of us to quickly acclimatise to the situation we were in. Looking at it from a rather technical point of view, they had encountered major tunnel complexes, in Cu Chi particularly, and they'd had to come to grips with that, with no special equipment. In fact, back in Australia the engineers went to the local shops and bought equipment to send up to 3 Field Troop to help them with tunnel search and clearance. So they'd certainly established a reputation for themselves as useful people to have around if you were going to bump into some tunnels.'

However, 3 Field Troop had already established that there were two sides to their collective character. 'Three Field Troop were well appreciated by the battalion, especially for the back-up they provided for the infantry,' recalls Warren. 'They had a reputation as being people who got things done. They also had a reputation for being people who worked hard and played hard and that was one area that had to be addressed to some extent.

'I had early discussions with Sandy about that aspect of it. There was no way that my whole squadron, with attachments getting on to 400 men, could maintain some of the attitudes, particularly towards play, that had prevailed in a smaller unit. So we both agreed it was a different ball game now. We were operating on new ground with new units, new people around us, and we had to set off the way we intended to proceed. Naturally, that would be different in some ways from the approach that had developed with 3 Field Troop but I hope I didn't do it heavy-handedly.'

Coming to 3 Field Troop fresh, Warren Lennon could see problems that even Sandy MacGregor and Geoff Stewart had failed to pick up on—probably due to the fact that gradual change is harder to spot when you see people every day.

'I can't underplay the fact that Sandy had soldiers who were shell-shocked,' recalls Warren. 'He had soldiers who were stressed from a lot of hard work and a lot of stressful situations and I had to make sure that stress was controlled, without mollycoddling them. Some of them had a few little personal hang-ups because they'd been having a pretty tough time, one way and another, and I didn't want their concerns to flow over. We also, as a new group, had to bring in some silly rules and some silly requirements that some of the fellas in 3 Troop couldn't accept as being very sensible . . .

'Is it sensible (as far as engineers are concerned) to arrive at the beginning of the wet season, trying to establish a task force in a rubber plantation? We had to try to build accommodation and roads and weapons pits and establish this whole mass of force in the middle of the monsoon. Prior to doing it, I would have said that was impossible, but we had to find ways. Now that really put massive pressure on my soldiers. They worked seven days a week, dawn to dusk every day. At first, I can't remember for how many weeks they had no stand-down time at all and I know that was not happily received by some of the soldiers and indeed some of the officers. From time to time I had to talk to people and say "Just go over and see the battalion wandering around in the mud and then tell me that you want to sit here and drink beer on a Sunday afternoon instead of getting on your dozer and going and helping them".'

Warren concedes the men were working very hard under very trying conditions and a few times he thought maybe he had pushed too hard. 'I had a padre ask me once why I didn't give my people some time off and I said we couldn't afford the time off,' he recalls. 'Then I thought, bloody hell, maybe we'd better.

'Another problem that was a major one, though it sounds silly, was that because there was a fairly high incidence of all kinds of malaria, one of the requirements was that people couldn't go out with their shirts off. If you're sitting on a great big D8 bulldozer on top of a very hot engine, you get a bit cranky if you've got to keep a shirt on in broad daylight. I required my soldiers to obey that rule. At the time, I thought if these fellows go down with malaria, then we can't do what we're here to do, so I insisted.

'So Sandy says "How would you like to be sitting on the dozer?" I said "I'll sit on the dozer but they'll wear their bloody shirts." He and I had some terse words from time to time about that issue, as I did with others. But they wore their shirts. They got frightful heat rash, many of them, and it finally reached the point where you were saying to yourself are they better to have this heat rash or should we run the risk of letting them get malaria? But we kept the shirts on.

'I remember one memorable day we had 60 soldiers all in a great big circle out in the sunshine with their shirts off dabbing each other's backs with calamine lotion and things to try and treat the heat rash. It was part of the medical parade.'

Sooner or later the discipline issue was bound to raise its head: 'The blokes in 3 Troop couldn't see why they shouldn't spend as much time at Vung Tau as they wanted to,' says Warren. 'That could have added some potential for concern. We were not in a position to be swanning off to Vung Tau but I think there were one or two occasions where people went anyhow. There were a couple, two or three, that were really in a bad position. They were shell-shocked. We decided we just had to get one of them out of the place because he was really at great risk. So I was conscious that these were battle-worn warriors, and not new recruits.'

Warren Lennon doesn't buy into the idea that the men of 3 Field Troop were hand-me-downs from other troops or soldiers the sergeants wanted to be rid of: 'Sandy had a few wild ones, but he was hardly a shrinking violet himself. He needed people like that. Forget the cast-offs theory; it was inevitable that some of those who volunteered would tend to be rather more adventurous and maybe a bit rougher than some of those who chose not to volunteer. They are natural adventurers and, as such, then they're probably prepared to challenge discipline and authority from time to time as well.'

For all that he was losing a little of his autonomy and there were tighter controls on the men, Sandy reckons Warren Lennon was a good boss who respected all the troop had achieved, and they worked out an ingenious way of teaming the veterans of 3 Troop with the new recruits so they would be able to train the sappers on the ground.

Every time they went out they had mini-teams of two with one of the 3 Troop boys as number one and one of the new boys as number two so that they worked together to pass on the knowledge to the new blokes in the field. From that day on, right through the whole of Australia's engineer involvement in Vietnam, that's how it was done. One Field Squadron stayed all the time, with individuals changing over, so that the experience gained wasn't removed, lock stock and barrel, when the battalions changed over (as happened with other units). There were a lot of mistakes made whenever new units arrived. The sappers couldn't afford to make mistakes.

So they were teaching as much as they could of their skills and running all sorts of courses on booby traps to get the new engineers familiar with them all. It was very much the end of an era. They were back in the mainstream of army life and they'd even lost the word 'Field' from 3 Field Troop, signifying that they were now just part of the much larger 1 Field Squadron. It wasn't their last adventure in Vietnam, but it required a big shift in their attitudes and priorities as more and more Australian troops arrived while they were already thinking of home.

# 16. PASSING THE BATON

The first 'real' operation under this new command was Operation Enoggera which ran from 21 June to 5 July and saw 3 Troop back in the tunnels in and around the village of Long Phuoc, just south-east of Nui Dat. The task force's tactical area of responsibility (TAOR) was an imaginary circle several kilometres out from Nui Dat, so any villages there had to be searched and cleared. After that, anyone found in that TAOR would either be the Allies, or the enemy.

Long Phuoc had been the scene of a large battle between American forces and the Vietcong back in May and had been the target of fairly substantial bombing and artillery fire since then. Village search and clearance meant having two engineers with every infantry section and the section corporal with a platoon commander. That meant that within a company of infantry there would be 18 to 20 engineers, plus the group at battalion to support them if they found a major system—a tunnel any longer than about 15 metres, for instance—so the engineer-supported infantry could keep on searching.

Interestingly, this meant that they often had corporals directly advising captains and even majors on what should be done in particular situations. It's to everyone's credit that the NCOs felt assured enough to offer advice and the officers felt confident enough to accept it. Enoggera was a big success for 1 Field Squadron and, being their first operation, was a major morale booster. Engineers discovered food, equipment and other Vietcong stores in tunnels and there were clear signs that the Vietcong had been there until soon before the engineers arrived, but there was very little contact with them. The engineers' mission was to destroy the villages and the tunnel systems so that the Vietcong couldn't come back too easily, so they were working flat-out for the whole 14 days.

The new men learned a few lessons the hard way. In one instance the infantry ventured down a tunnel, with one idiot lighting his way with a flare. Had he been on Crimp, he'd have known the fatal consequences for anyone coming after you when the oxygen has all been burned up. Another act of blatant stupidity was when the infantry torched an abandoned hut while there were sappers in the tunnels underneath it. They could have been burned, asphyxiated or blown up with their own explosives, for all the grunts up top knew or cared. As Warren Lennon said in his report at the time, it didn't inspire much confidence.

It was during Enoggera that Australian troops were accused of using gas warfare against the Vietcong. 'We were always looking for new and more effective ways to destroy tunnels so we decided to try this new machine which had just arrived from Australia,' explains Sandy. 'It was a jet engine that blew a mist of diesel and air into the tunnel (after we'd searched it, of course). When the tunnel was full the mist was ignited and it would blow up the tunnel. It didn't really work but Pat Burgess, the famous Australian newspaper journalist, was out there with us at the time and he wrote about this fantastic new invention which blew "gas" into the tunnels.'

Meanwhile 3 Troop were teaching tunnel search techniques to new arrivals, and in one tunnel they found kerosene tins piled one on top of another, hiding an entrance to a room. It was new arrival 'Rocky' Rockcliffe's first tunnel, so they let him carry the rifles out and there was someone waiting with a camera, to capture the moment for posterity.

That picture accompanied the newspaper article by Pat Burgess that led to Australia being accused of using gas warfare. The Swedish government objected to 'gas warfare' and ordered their arms industry to stop supplying us with arms, ammunition and spare parts for our M-79 rocket launcher known as the Carl Gustav.

'I became good friends with Pat after Vietnam and he always insisted that he had been using the American meaning of the word "gas"—that is, petrol or fuel,' says Sandy. 'Anyway, the story was somehow sent back to Europe and the next thing we knew we had a full-scale diplomatic incident on our hands. In fact it was no more gas warfare than slinging tear gas down the hole, and the Yanks had been doing that from day one—but that's politics.'

Both of 3 Troop's last two operations, Sydney (7-23 July) and Holsworthy (9-18 August), were similar search-and-destroy operations. They were long and hard, but at least this time 3 Troop weren't working alone. They had 1 Troop to share their load as they passed on the benefits of many months in the field.

They also had to work up a completely new relationship with the infantry, and now had two infantry commanders to deal with. One of these—Lieutenant Colonel Waugh of 5 RAR—wanted to use his assault pioneers to clear booby traps and the like, and to provide the close support that was given to the infantry in the field. An assault pioneer is basically a hybrid of engineer and infanteer, and some infantry commanders preferred to use them rather than calling engineers in.

More often than not, they were asked to deal with wires, mines, booby traps and construction of their weapons pits and couldn't be expected to be trained to the level that the engineers were. But there were assault pioneers in 1 RAR who were just as keen to get their hands dirty as the sappers, so they could have been putting pressure on their commanders. While the engineers were discovering underground cities, the assault pioneers were stuck back at battalion HQ digging weapons pits.

'Suffice it to say that when the new infantry commanders arrived, one of them liked the way we worked and one of them, for his own reasons, didn't,' says Sandy, who admits he pushed hard for his lads to be involved as much as possible. 'It was his loss.'

Operation Holsworthy, 3 Troop's last operation, ended on 18 August 1966. That's a memorable date in Australian military history: it was the date of the battle of Long Tan and although 3 Troop weren't directly involved, they didn't miss out altogether. Far from it . . .

# 17. THE LONG NIGHT BEFORE LONG TAN

On the second-last day of Operation Holsworthy, 17 August 1966, 3 Troop were north of Nui Dat, continuing their search-and-clear operations near a village called Binh Bah. This was 3 Troop's second-biggest operation after New Life, bigger even than Crimp, and was their farewell to the jungles of Vietnam. Little did they know it was also close to being a permanent farewell to them and their new comrades.

Their base camp was mortared and most of the shots landed in the 1 Field Squadron area. The next day, D Company of 6 RAR was sent out to replace B Company to continue the investigation of what they assumed were a small number of guerrillas. Instead, about 5 kilometres east of Nui Dat, they stumbled into the Vietcong 274th Regiment supported by regulars from the North Vietnamese Army and D445 Battalion.

What followed was one of the most heroic passages in Australian military history. Surrounded, and out of ammunition, D Company hung on until night when, just as all seemed lost, Australian armoured personnel carriers and infantrymen forced their way through the enemy lines to relieve them. Attacking from behind the enemy, with the monsoon rain drowning out the noise from their vehicles, the APCs arrived like the proverbial cavalry and drove the enemy off.

The next day would dawn on 17 Australian dead and 27 wounded while 245 North Vietnamese bodies were found in the surrounding jungle amid signs that many more seriously wounded men had been dragged away by their comrades. One hundred and eight Australians had held off about 2500 enemy, aided by pinpoint Anzac artillery strikes and the fearless Aussie chopper pilots who had supplied ammunition in the midst of the firestorm, with little visibility.

The members of 3 Troop who were with 1 Field Squadron on Operation Holsworthy were about 10 kilometres away from all this, aware of what was happening only because of the radio traffic they were picking up. But back in camp, they were preparing themselves for an onslaught. Their positions were the weak point in the defences. If the enemy could drive through 1 Field Squadron's lines (actually the gap between

6 RAR and 1 Field Squadron, the exact location that 3 Field Troop occupied and overlooked when they first arrived at Nui Dat) they'd be straight into the Australian Task Force's headquarters.

North Vietnamese prisoners captured after Long Tan revealed that the plan was to hit Nui Dat the next morning. The Vietcong had detailed maps showing the weak points in the Australian defences. Had they not encountered the men from D Company, they would have waded through.

'Considering that most of the sappers would have been exhausted after a nine-day operation, and my lot, at least, demob happy, I can't see how it would have been a very pleasant time,' observes Sandy. 'The Vietcong plan was to take out the task force HQ. We were the only thing in their way.'

The lads back in camp knew something was up the previous day, when the first of the mortar shells rained in on their positions. Mick McGrath, Les Colmer, Snow Wilson and Sandy Saunders were all among those left behind and they all have vivid memories of those crucial 24 hours.

'I knew something was wrong—three days ahead, I knew,' says Les Colmer. 'Most of the troop was out, and I had a bung wrist at the time so they stuck me in the store. I think Meggsie Dennis was in the store and he had an Owen gun and he said "I'm going out and you're taking my place. Can I swap my Owen gun for your rifle?" But as soon as they left camp I just knew it, something was up, and for three days I was ratshit.

'There were about four or five of us in our area of the camp when the Vietcong mortared us. There were about five or six shells in a row. There's not much you can do when you're being mortared. Just shake and shiver and try to make it to the shithouse as soon as it stops.'

Mick McGrath reckons he shouldn't even have been in Nui Dat, and not because he should have been with the rest of the troop. He'd had prickly heat rashes which had turned very nasty and the doctor had wanted to send him back to Australia, but Sandy said he didn't have enough men as it was and couldn't afford to lose any more—was there any alternative?

'I had five days down at Vung Tau, swimming in the salt water three times a day for a week, and then I went back up to Nui Dat,' Mick recalls. 'I wasn't pushed into going bush, I was kept back at base camp to help defend our area, plus other daily chores, so that we could keep as many men as we could out in the field, helping the new blokes work their way into our methods. The night before Long Tan I was in camp there and my tent was the closest one to the wire where the Vietcong were heading. I had the machine gun and I had all me clickers there ready to set off all the Claymores out in front.

'Anyway, the mortars came in and I heard Lieutenant Stewart yelling out everybody's name, 'cause he had to know everybody that was in there and there was about 16 of us. Anyway, Van Ham never answered and I said I'd go and check. So

I'm running around looking for Van and I couldn't find him. I said I couldn't look any more. I had to go back because we knew an attack always followed mortars, so I went back and stayed in me weapon pit.

'Later on in the night Gus Sant came around checking up on everybody and I asked him if he'd found Van and he said he was all right. But there were three tents pretty extensively damaged from the mortars and some shrapnel came through my tent. Peter Ash's tent took a direct hit—just as well he was out on Operation Holsworthy. But if it hadn't have been for that torrential rain I would probably be looking down the teeth of a couple of hundred of 'em. And you wouldn't have seen them until they were probably 30 or 40 metres away from you—in the dark that wouldn't have been much help to you at all. It was eerie how close we came to really copping it.

'We were just lucky that the rain slowed 'em down and then D Company happened to be in the wrong place at the right time for us and took the whole brunt of the attack, otherwise it would have been heading our way. Just like we were blessed, wasn't it?'

For Snow Wilson, after the trauma of the camp being mortared, Long Tan was a remote experience. It was only a few kilometres through the jungles, but all he knew was what he heard over the radio.

'We were working within the task force area,' says Snow. 'On the night of Long Tan I went over to the Pioneer Platoon, who were just across the road from our section. I had a couple of beers over there and we sat and listened to the battle of Long Tan on one of the infantry radios.'

It was a strange experience for most of the troop to be so close to history and yet scarcely be a part of it. Were the Vietcong planning to attack on the 17th? If not, why did they give themselves away by firing their mortars 24 hours earlier when normally an attack follows immediately? Were they, as Mick McGrath believes, planning to attack there and then, but slowed down by the rain? Maybe, as he says, they were blessed. Otherwise they'd have been history . . . literally.

# 18. THE LAST POST

The last days 3 Troop spent in Nui Dat were a bit of an anticlimax. The task force was pursuing the attackers from Long Tan as they tried to get back to safer territory, and the sappers were working flat-out to improve the facilities around the camp, building roads and extending the airport. The lads were desperately looking forward to going home. As Warren Lennon had noted, many of them were shell-shocked or at least psychologically shaken up. And there is hardly one who hasn't said that without doubt the best thing that happened to them was flying home.

Sandy MacGregor elected to stay on for another month to observe the American engineers, so the troop's farewell parade in September 1966 was as much a farewell to him as it was to Vietnam.

'As we stood there in our best kit on a parade ground we had built for 1 Field Squadron, 1 Battalion Commander Brigadier Jackson came to see us off. It was he who took my side at Vung Tau and overruled the major who wanted to stick us five miles away up the beach, so it was only appropriate that he should be there to say farewell to the men. I can't remember exactly what he said but it was along the lines of: "I look forward to serving with you all again some day . . . but never again all at the same time."'

The blokes loved it. Brigadier Jackson clearly recognised their immense capabilities and realised that not even the horrors of Vietnam could quell their larrikin spirit. And when all the speeches were over, he saluted the men of 3 Field Troop as they marched together for the last time, across a dusty parade ground and into a half-forgotten corner of military history.

When the blokes went home, Sandy went to 65th Engineer Battalion, 25 Division, which was at Cu Chi, to get experience of a battalion of engineers, which is like having three squadrons of engineers in one place, something he'd never known.

'In that time I went out to have a look at the tunnels which were outside Cu Chi,' says Sandy. 'They were tiny little sand tunnels which were too dangerous to search. They were just the bits and pieces and I think the Vietnamese were just training themselves, they were just like hidey-holes. But eventually the whole of 65th Engineers had tunnels coming underneath them into the base. And, more interestingly, I am sure they connected up with the tunnels we found in Ho Bo Woods. The former Vietnamese commander says there are hundreds of kilometres of tunnels, so it's entirely possible.'

Two days before he got back to Nui Dat, Sandy was telephoned by Warren Lennon, who said: 'Congratulations, MacGregor, you've been awarded the Military Cross.'

'I wasn't the only one to win a medal,' says Sandy. 'The whole troop won a US Meritorious Unit Commendation (MUC), along with the rest of 1 RAR Group and 173rd Airborne Brigade, which the present day's 3 Troop (plus all the original members of 3 Field Troop) is allowed to wear as a permanent feature of their uniform. The ribbon is red in colour, it's bound by a gold metal edge and worn on the right breast pocket. The Americans also gave me a Bronze Star and they awarded young Tommy Mason an Army Commendation Medal for Meritorious Service—I assume for all the sterling work he did in the tunnels.

'And I wasn't the only Australian in Vietnam with 1 RAR to deserve a Military Cross—not by a long shot. Captain Bob Hill, the APC commander with the Prince of Wales Light Horse, also received one but there were many more soldiers with

I RAR who should have won an MC but who were deprived by stupid military bureaucracy.

'You see, it was decided that there would only be two MCs awarded per battalion, per year. Why you would want to set a limit like that is beyond me. Then they decided that for the purposes of military decorations I RAR group would be counted as the battalion. The commanding officer of I RAR group put their recommendations in early for engineers and armour—that was for me and Bob—while for I RAR it was decided to sit on their recommendations until a little later.

'Quite reasonably, they wanted to pick the best of the bunch. But that was a mistake. Before they knew it, Bob and I had won our medals and the battalion was told "That's your lot" as far as I RAR goes. Now, I'm not saying I didn't deserve the Military Cross, and I definitely know that Bob deserved his, but I also know for a fact that there were a lot of men in the infantry who deserved the Military Cross too. Once again, thanks to the pen-pushers, the front-line soldier lost out.'

Sandy is quick to honour the men who served under him in Vietnam. He recommended Peter Ash, Tommy Mason, Barry Harford, Doug Sanderson, Les Colmer and Bill Gallagher for a variety of decorations including the Military Medal (MM), Mentioned in Despatches (MID), and the Queen's Commendation. Unfortunately they weren't awarded.

'No one knew they'd been nominated,' he says. 'Military protocol demands secrecy—but now the secret's out.'

Some of his troop went on to have distinguished military careers. Dennis Ayoub rose through the ranks and reached major by the time he retired. John Opie also retired as a major and Tex Cotter turned out to be officer material too. Bill Corby, Jack Fairweather, Bill Gallagher, Brian Hay, Carl Richards, Gus Sant, Ross Thorburn, Billy Unmeopa, Snow Wilson and Ray Wilson all made warrant officer in the regular Army.

At the end of his tour of duty in Vietnam, Sandy MacGregor was posted to the School of Military Engineering as Captain Instructor, Operations. It was a plum posting, and allowed him to use his experiences to help train young officers, most of whom were to serve in Vietnam. He spent his last night in Vietnam hitting the bars of Saigon with Bob Musgrove, who was in the Armoured Corps in the Australian Army HQ, had been in his class at Duntroon and was the best man at his first wedding.

Years later he met Bob again. Bob had made a study of traumatic stress syndrome—something that used to be called 'shell shock'—and they discussed the effect that the year in Vietnam had on the members of the troop and other veterans in general.

'He pointed out that even in the Second World War the troops were never subjected to the kinds of stresses we had to endure in Vietnam,' says Sandy. 'In the Second World War, blokes would be fighting at the front for a week or a month or however long they were needed, but then they were relieved by other troops. And when they left the Front, they'd go somewhere completely safe, where they'd be able to go on leave, be among friends, totally relax and retrain, if need be.

'It wasn't like that in Vietnam. The guys would go out on operations, then they'd come back to a base camp, where they still had to mount guard and do their duties and other works. Even when they had a day's leave in Saigon or Vung Tau, it was a day spent among enemy—you never knew for sure which side anybody was on, but you did know for sure that there were Vietcong among the crowds.

'As Bob pointed out, there was stress at every moment. It was a more consistent stress in Vietnam. And that, he said, contributed to traumatic stress syndrome.'

Sandy's younger brother Chris—an engineer corporal with 1 Field Squadron—was involved in the worst landmine disaster in Vietnam, in the Long Hai Hills on 28 February 1970 on Operation Hamersley, when booby traps killed nine and wounded 15 soldiers (including one engineer dead and one wounded).

'When Chris got over there he had to search and identify most of the dead,' says Sandy. 'He also had to make the path safe to go to the guys who were wounded. But strangely, he has hardly any memory of that. All he could remember for a long time was barren rock and very dry ground. To me, it's very possible that this is a sign of traumatic stress syndrome, but Chris would laugh off the very idea. When I think back to 1966, I probably would have laughed it off too if someone had suggested I was suffering from traumatic stress.

'But now that I work at helping people to develop the power of their subconscious minds, I would never dismiss out of hand any suggestion that those who have been deeply traumatised may have suffered lasting effects. Looking at the guys from 3 Troop who have claimed over the years to have been affected, I can only say that they have my support, for what it's worth.'

Heroic acts and what often passes for bravery can seem merely foolhardy in a different light; courage should not be confused with the reckless tempting of fate. The men of 3 Field Troop had a job to do and they did it with courage, skill and enthusiasm and saved the crazy stuff for the bars of Saigon, Bien Hoa and Vung Tau.

You could argue that they benefitted from being the first to go down the tunnels—maybe they would have been less enthusiastic if they'd known what was down there. But that doesn't stack up when you read their stories of courage and commitment, especially after Bob Bowtell died.

The men of 3 Field Troop were followed by many other brave soldiers—Australian and American—and they may have called themselves 'tunnel ferrets' to an uncomprehending American press. But the simple fact remains: they were Tunnel Rats and they were the originals.

# APPENDIX A

## THE TUNNELS OF VIETNAM

If you go to Cu Chi these days, a short drive from Saigon city centre, you can go down a tunnel system, fire a range of weaponry and watch a documentary about the tunnels and the conflict that the Vietnamese call the 'American War'. But it's not real. The tunnels have been widened and their ceilings raised to accommodate overgrown and overfed Western tourists, the guns—from a Colt 45 pistol to a huge belt-fed machine gun—fire real bullets but at metal targets, rather than people, and the propaganda in the documentary is so over the top it sounds like a Monty Python spoof: 'the traitor puppets of the American imperialist running dogs' get a few dishonourable mentions. It's true what they say: history is written by the winners.

The display that shocks Western tourists the most is the museum of booby traps. Confronted by the array of fiendishly clever bombs, spikes and destructive devices, I heard one Australian murmur, 'We never stood a chance . . .' Certainly the Vietcong did something from day one that the Americans failed to do until it was too late . . . they tried to understand their enemy and then adapted their methods accordingly. The Australians were so effective, and respected by their foes, because they too adapted to the fact that this was a different kind of war against a different kind of foe. These days the description of the Vietnam War is an 'asymmetric' conflict—David versus Goliath, if you wish. But when it came to the Vietcong fighting Australians, it was more like David versus David.

Several times in this book we have referred to the tunnels as being the Vietcong's secret weapon, and it's an entirely valid description. The tunnels themselves weren't a secret for long but their extent, complexity and strategic function were. As for being a weapon, and a very powerful one, of that there is no doubt; think of them as a fleet of underground submarines, if you like, and you get a sense of their potential threat.

In *The Tunnels of Cu Chi*, the definitive book about the US investigations of the tunnels *after* 3 Field Troop had led the way underground, Tom Mangold and John Penycate write: 'The underground tunnels of Cu Chi were the most complex part of a network that, at the height of the Vietnam War in the mid-sixties, stretched from the gates of Saigon to the border with Cambodia. There were hundreds of kilometres of tunnels connecting villages, districts, and even provinces. They held living areas, storage depots, ordnance factories, hospitals, headquarters, and almost every other facility that was necessary to the pursuit of the war by South Vietnam's communists and that could be accommodated below ground.'

As a defensive installation, it was brilliantly effective. The tunnels were designed so that they could be sealed off in small sections that limited the effects from bombs, smoke and tear gas. Troops lived underground for months at a time and, although conditions were less than healthy, it was safer than being shot at or bombed. The Cu Chi tunnels went down six levels and included everything required to keep an army fed, watered and occupied.

There were classrooms for weapons instructions and tactical lessons. There were bomb-making rooms where trash discarded by Allied troops—mostly the Americans—would be turned into booby traps. The irony of converting a dumped Coca-Cola can into a small bomb was not lost on the Vietcong—or the Australians, who soon worked out that any material they left behind in the field might one day be used against them.

There were hospitals where wounded could be treated, and culverts dug into the sides of the tunnel where they could be safely left, without blocking free movement along the passages, while the battle raged on above them.

Field kitchens had cleverly designed chimneys so that the smoke from them was dissipated then came out far away from the kitchen itself. Entrances—carefully spaced far enough apart so that the discovery of one didn't lead to the uncovering of all of them—were often in river banks, allowing the troops to come and go without ever being on dry land.

Air vents were concealed under bushes and behind rocks. Hides for snipers, like the one employed so murderously at the start of Operation Crimp, were cunningly concealed within earth mounds and anthills. So these tunnels weren't so much underground cities as subterranean fortresses. As Appendix B reveals, a lot of thought went into the design and construction of the tunnels but, again, it wasn't a textbook approach based on theory. These practicalities had been arrived at over decades of fighting superior forces: the French, the Japanese, the French again, then the Americans and their allies. The development of the tunnels was deliberate yet organic so that by the time the National Liberation Front (Vietcong) and the North Vietnamese army were ready for the final push against the Allies, the knowledge acquired over decades of tunnel warfare had enabled the Vietcong to build a sophisticated series of underground complexes linked by hundreds of kilometres of passages.

And that is one of the most remarkable things about this amazing feat of civil and military engineering: no one ordered it to be built. There was no master plan, no great vision and no single driving force behind it. The tunnels evolved as the only possible response by an ill-equipped guerrilla army to helicopter gunships, carpet-bombing raids and massive artillery fire. And their uses weren't purely defensive. They not only allowed the North Vietnamese to hold out against vastly superior forces for much longer, they provided an unseen base for sustained assaults. Troops, munitions and supplies could be moved over large distances without being detected. They could also be held in reserve in case reinforcements were needed or brought out to attack in typical guerrilla hit-and-run operations.

Estimates of the maximum capacity of the Cu Chi tunnels differ, but various reports from the North have suggested that between 5000 and 10,000 men and women were secreted underground at various times. Whatever the figure, that's a lot of fighters to be able to put on the ground—and then just as quickly make disappear—without your enemy even being aware that they are around. But knowing about the tunnels, as the Allies eventually did, and doing something about them were two very different issues.

In Operation Cedar Falls in 1967, some 30,000 troops (as opposed to fewer than 10,000 involved in Crimp) embarked on a more determined assault on Cu Chi and the so-called

Iron Triangle, the general area where the Vietcong were particularly strong. Better-equipped US Tunnel Rats uncovered the Vietcong district headquarters in the Cu Chi tunnels and brought out half a million documents, among which were maps of US bases, lists of political sympathisers, and assassination plans.

Even so, the mission was otherwise considered a failure, as demonstrated when the Cu Chi complex was the strategic headquarters for the North's Tet Offensive in 1968, which was intended to lead to a general uprising in the South. That campaign's greatest achievement was to change public opinion in America and Australia, where the view had been propagated that the North's forces were weak and easily subdued. Militarily, the Tet Offensive was a flop, but in the battle for hearts and minds of the people of Australia and America, the North had scored a major victory. And as the tunnels crept ever closer to Saigon, sometimes going right beneath the Allied forces' camps, attempts to blast them to oblivion—B-52s returning from missions to the North were encouraged to drop any remaining bombs onto Cu Chi—had only limited effect, and the tunnels were still in use right up to the final assault on Saigon.

If tunnel missions were tough for Allied soldiers, life underground was far from pleasant for their foes. Air quality was an obvious major concern and food and water were often rationed. The tunnels were infested with poisonous insects and mosquitoes, and their inhabitants rarely saw daylight, emerging only at night to scavenge for food, tend their crops or fight. It was a desperately unhealthy existence. One Vietcong report suggested that at any given time half of a tunnel-bound unit would have malaria and that all of them had intestinal parasites. Malaria had the second-highest death toll in the tunnels after wounds sustained in battle.

But it was Vietnamese industry and ingenuity that prevailed. They had electricity underground, thanks to pedal and hand generators, discarded American batteries and, in one case, a captured battle tank that was dug into a tunnel complex to be used as a command centre. In some of the deeper levels there were reports of workshops and storerooms big enough to service and store field guns which were dismantled every night and taken underground—explaining why the Allies could never work out where the shelling was coming from.

There was also evidence discovered of workshops where skilled tradesmen were creating exact working replicas of captured guns and rifles. Who knew the fashion knock-off business had such a deadly precursor?

While the Iron Triangle area around Cu Chi was the obvious target of ant-tunnelling activities, there were other tunnel systems elsewhere, some of which had purely defensive roles. In Vinh Moc, on the border between North and South Vietnam, the tunnels were built to shelter locals from intense bombing intended to prevent them from supplying food and armaments to the North Vietnamese garrison on the island of Con Co, which was attacking American bombers on their way to bomb Hanoi.

Villagers initially dug tunnels so they could live underground but the Americans designed bombs that burrowed down 10 metres before exploding. Typically, the response was to go even further down—up to 30 metres and three levels—to escape the tunnel bombs. Like the military tunnels at Cu Chi, the Vinh Moc complex included wells, kitchens, bedrooms and medical facilities. About 60 families lived in the tunnels and about 20 children were born there between 1966 and 1972.

The tourist tunnels at Cu Chi only give a flavour of the reality behind them. The real tunnels spread for hundreds of kilometres and went down half a dozen levels. The rooms varied from scrapings in the tunnel wall to vaults 5 metres high. But how effective were they? History records that Australian troops started pulling out of Vietnam in 1970 and were gone by 1973, as were the American forces. Saigon and the South finally fell to North Vietnamese forces on 30 April 1975. A vastly out-gunned combination of regular army and guerrilla forces had defeated the combined might of South Vietnam, America, South Korea, Australia, New Zealand, the Philippines and Thailand in a war that lasted 19 years and 170 days.

Maybe, just maybe, if American forces in the early days had done what 3 Field Troop did, at the first opportunity, the effectiveness of the tunnels would have been nullified and there could have been a very different outcome.

# APPENDIX B

## HOW TO BUILD AN UNDERGROUND CITY

As described elsewhere in this book, the effective tactical deployment of tunnel warfare evolved over many years, but there is no evidence to suggest that there was ever a 'master plan' to build the networks of tunnels in the form that they eventually took.

However, it's clear from the following document—discovered by Korean forces in September 1967 and translated into English long after 3 Field Troop had been and gone—that having realised the strategic value of their tunnels, the North Vietnamese weren't keen to leave anything to chance.

This document is basically a 'how to' training booklet on tunnel planning, building and operations, outlining the preferred design of tunnels and discussing their uses, construction, specifications and maintenance.

It details everything from the size of the entrances and their positions relative to each other to the numbers in digging teams and what they should do with the soil they pull out of the ground. It also reveals how important the tunnel systems were to the Vietcong, referring frequently to the reason for their existence being simply that they were outgunned by the Allies.

The document gives us a remarkable insight into the thinking behind the tunnels. These days, knowing the commitment, ingenuity and industry of Vietnamese people, it's little wonder that they had made a science out of their construction, location and operation.

## Construction of Underground Tunnels in Combat Villages and Hamlets

### FOREWORD

Underground tunnels have existed for a long time, and their construction requires special building techniques. No documents on this subject, however, have ever been issued. Recently, the task of digging underground tunnels depended mainly upon the ability of the people in local areas. As a result, the methods adopted were different and the effectiveness of underground tunnels was highly variable.

In some local areas, the underground tunnel met the required conditions as expected; in other areas, however, their role was misunderstood. Because of the people's lack of basic technical knowledge, the tunnels were either unusable after much manpower had been expended or became mere shelters instead of strong combat posts.

This document compiles the basic technique of construction with the experience gained in local areas. Its purpose is to provide technical assistance for combat villages and hamlets. I will exclude all tactical matters. Though the document refers to the experiences gained in many different places, it is still far from adequate. We expect to see it enriched with more suggestions and ideas from the local areas and from various units.

## I. The role and effectiveness of Engineer Section underground tunnels in combat villages and hamlets

### 1. The role of underground tunnels:

The war has become increasingly fierce. The enemy is trying to paralyse our combat potential with intensive air and artillery attacks. In the face of this situation, we should realise the necessity of the people's warfare. We must overcome all difficulties in order to intensify guerrilla activities in support of a war of movement.

The primary role of underground tunnels is the strengthening of combat vitality for our villages. They also provide more safety for our political and armed units, and for the masses as well. But their sheltering purpose is only significant when they serve our soldiers in combat activities. As mere shelters, their great advantages are wasted. Their construction should therefore be in accordance with the combat plan as drafted by the villages and hamlets. There should be combat posts and equipment inside the underground tunnels for providing continuous support to our troops even if the enemy occupies the village. The armed forces must be able to enter one passage of the underground tunnels and exit from another or disappear and appear suddenly in order to attack the enemy.

Furthermore, we should plan for the eventual impossibility of fighting from inside the underground tunnels. A secret passage must then be available from which our troops may escape and fight in the open, or re-enter the underground tunnels, if necessary.

2. The effectiveness of underground tunnels :

a) **They strengthen the combat vitality of villages and hamlets:** If the underground tunnels are dug so as to exploit their effectiveness fully, the villages and hamlets will become extremely strong fortresses. The enemy may be several times superior to us in strength and modern weapons, but he will not chase us from the battlefield, because we will launch surprise attacks from within the underground tunnels. We can see then that underground tunnels are very favourable for armed forces as limited as are ours in strength and weaponry.

b) **They reduce the advantage the enemy has, of superior firepower:** Effective underground tunnels help our forces launch close-in attacks on the enemy, while providing opportunities for the seizure of weapons.

c) **They enable our forces to wear down the enemy's potential with relatively few weapons.**

d) **They provide more mobility for our troops:** We may attack the enemy right in the centre of his formations or keep on fighting from different places.

II. <u>Influence of the terrain upon underground tunnels</u>

The terrain in different areas may influence the underground tunnels differently according to the undercurrents, nature of the soil in this document: Midland and mountain areas; Lowland and populated areas

<u>1. Midland and mountain areas:</u>

Digging underground tunnels in midland and mountain areas often takes much time, manpower and materials, because there are a great deal of rocks, and tree roots. But the tunnels in these areas are strong. We need few supporting poles, and water is more easily drained.

<u>2. Lowland and populated areas:</u>

The soil in these areas is usually soft and saturated with water. In the rainy season, the earth can slide. There must be many poles set up to support the tunnels, so the cost of materials is correspondingly higher. In sandy areas, there must be frames for supporting the roof and walls of the underground tunnel, and covers for the openings (in lowland and coastal areas). The most difficult problem is that of draining water and strengthening the tunnels against landslides. This should be given particular notice, if we wish to render the underground tunnels most effective.

III. <u>Basic principles of the construction of underground tunnels</u>:

The construction of underground tunnels must be based on the following principles: the terrain where the underground tunnel is dug; the enemy situation; the friendly situation.

<u>1. Terrain:</u>

The terrain directly affects our combat activities and tactics as well as the cost of manpower and materials. There must be a careful selection of the terrain before the construction of underground tunnels is begun. This is an important precaution to consider in our preparatory work.

<u>2. The enemy situation:</u>

The main purpose of the underground tunnel is to increase our combat capability. The enemy has always tried to destroy our underground tunnels. Some local areas, however, made very little use of their underground tunnels, though they had invested a great deal of manpower and materials to their construction. They ignored the enemy situation and failed to coordinate the effectiveness of underground tunnels with combat plans when the enemy attacked. They should have studied the enemy's operating methods and possibilities of attack before beginning the construction of underground tunnels. NB: Lessons should be drawn from the enemy's previous sweep operations.

3. The friendly situation:

The digging of underground tunnels must be carried out in accordance with the organisation and equipment of the village and hamlet militia and guerrilla units. All the possibilities of manoeuvring manpower and providing materials and tools must be considered and planned beforehand.

IV. Principles, technical requirements and distribution of work

A. Principles

In order to maintain security and prevent the enemy from discovering and destroying our underground tunnels, the following principles must be observed:

- Select an appropriate location for the underground tunnel.
- Determine the location of the entrance into the underground tunnel.
- Determine the location of the angles and passages in the underground tunnel.

1. How to select the location:

a) The underground tunnel must be located where it serves combat activities most effectively. It is constructed more for combat than for shelter purposes. If it fails to meet the actual requirements of the situation, it will create difficulties for our soldiers.

b) Select dry areas or places where the water table is very deep underground. Elevated areas are most preferable, because flooded, damp areas will require much manpower, time and materials and the underground tunnel will be subject to slides and cave-ins.

c) Select easily camouflaged areas: secrecy is an important factor in rendering the underground tunnel strong and effective. Secrecy also provides opportunities for launching surprise attacks.

Well-camouflaged areas protect our soldiers from detection by the enemy. NB: Camouflage should by no means disturb the movement of our troops in combat.

**2. Entrance into the underground tunnel:**

a) Pre-construction tasks: The soil selected for underground tunnels in lowlands should preferably be mixed with gravel and rocks, because it will save on manpower and time. Furthermore, the cadre in charge of selecting the location should examine the terrain carefully.

b) Secrecy and surprise: Surprise is an extremely important factor in the war against the enemy. We continually try to destroy the enemy, and he does likewise to us. While selecting the location, the cadre must take into consideration both future combat activities and the surprise factor that enables us to attack the enemy without being detected by him.

c) Possibilities for raids: Because the activities of the militia and guerrillas require appearing and disappearing quickly, the entrances to the underground tunnel must be located like the corners of a triangle, so that each can support the other in combat. Our troops must be also able to escape from the underground tunnel, through a secret opening, so they may continue to fight.

d) Measures against floods and asphyxia: As we know, the US Imperialists make use of highly lethal weapons in order to kill us and attain their vicious end. They drop explosives and incendiary bombs, and even pour chemicals into our underground tunnels. For this reason, we must locate the entrances to the tunnels in dry, elevated and well-ventilated areas. Such an entrance will not be blocked by the chemicals that will otherwise kill the occupants. Also, rain water will not stagnate in an entrance so located.

3. Corners and passages in the underground tunnels:

a) Corners: The passages in the underground tunnels must not all be straight or snake-like. They must be made in 60° and 120° angles; that is, not less than 60° but not more than 120°.

b) The passages: They must be neither too broad nor too narrow. The nature of the soil as well as the strength of troops using them must be studied before they are dug. Underground passages should not be dug underneath common paths, because the enemy will discover them easily.

4. Thickness of the roof:

The minimum thickness of the roof must be 1.5 metres, if we wish to avoid vibration caused by the explosions of bombs and shells, and the sounds of mechanised units moving above.

# APPENDIX B

B. Technical requirements and distribution of work

**1. The different parts and the technical requirements:**

a) Entrance: It must be hidden and easily camouflaged; it must serve combat activities; it must be favourable for our fields of fire; it must have accurate dimensions.

- **It must be hidden and easily camouflaged:** The construction of underground tunnel entrances has been misunderstood recently in some local areas. They dug the entrances in open areas, possibly to help the diggers remove the earth more rapidly. They did not realise the importance of secrecy. Their carelessness enabled the enemy to discover the underground tunnel easily. We should therefore dig hidden, easily camouflaged entrances to ensure safety for our soldiers and weapons.
- **It must serve combat activities:** Though the technical side of digging entrances is important, the tactical side should not be disregarded. We noted that most underground tunnel entrances in local areas were not located as they could support each other. They were dug in straight lines. The cause for the error was that they were regarded more as a place for exit and entrance than as a fortification for success in combat. The entrances must be located in triangular form. The distance between two entrances depends upon the firing range of their defenders. The average distance is 40 to 50 metres.
- **Distance between the entrances:** In some local areas, the

entrances were located only a small distance from each other. They were only 10 to 12 metres apart. Worse still, in some places, they were just 5 to 7 metres apart. The reason was that the digging was entrusted to separate families or groups of persons, who could not foresee the disastrous effects of their thoughtlessness. Though a number of entrances were later filled up, we noted that this deficiency has been carried over in many other local areas. They seem to ignore the fact that close entrances attract the enemy's attention and do nothing but assist his discovery.

As far as actual experience has taught us, the distance between two entrances should be at least 20 to 30 metres. Difficulties will certainly arise, because at such a great distance, the diggers may deviate from the planned direction and their output may be reduced. But we gain the advantage of maintaining the secrecy of our underground tunnels.

- **Accurate dimensions**: The entrance of an underground tunnel must be strong. We need to expend a great deal of manpower, time and materials to make it so. The following dimensions are to be adopted:

| | |
|---|---|
| —Square entrance | 1.5 metres for each side |
| —Rectangular entrances | 1 metre × 1.8 metres |
| —Round entrances | 1.5 metres in diameter. |

Recently, local areas have observed no systematic digging procedure. Some entrances were too large and remained weak; thus time, manpower and materials had been wasted. The local people tried to correct the blunder, but their hasty work caused additional earth to cave in and help the enemy discover the entrance. Small entrances are stronger but they disturb our movement and render entering or exiting difficult. In short, both large and small entrances are ineffective. We therefore recommend the above dimensions, which we hope will be studied and utilised by all local areas.

b) The passages: The following requirements must be met if we wish to allow safe and successful fighting from the underground passages:

—The passages must not be wider than 1.2 metres
—They must not be narrower than 0.8 m
—They must not be higher than 1.8 m
—They must not be lower than 0.8 m
—Their angles must not be smaller than 60°
—Their angles must not be larger than 120°
—Their directions must be accurate
—They must have by-passages and several floors.

- **Why must they be neither wide and high, nor narrow and low?** Digging wide, high passages requires much time and manpower. Such passages are usually weak; they shake or cave in when disturbed by bomb and shell explosions. Low, narrow passages, on the other hand, save time and manpower, but they disturb the movement of troops and affect our combat activities. We can therefore conclude that the size of the passage depends on the nature of the soil, the number of troops occupying the underground tunnel and the possibilities of troop movement. The above dimensions are expected to be the most favourable.

- **Why must they be dug in a zigzag fashion?** Most local areas have recently made the passages of their underground tunnels snake-like, or even in straight lines. This is dangerous, because if the enemy detects the entrance to the underground tunnel, he will set off mines and bangalores [extended tube bombs] or pour in chemicals, both of which are certain to have disastrous effects on our troops. This is why we must dig the passages in a zigzag fashion and provide covers at the corners and between the floors.
- **Why are by-passages and floors necessary?** Probably because they were entrusted task work and wanted to build their underground tunnel more quickly, or because of a lack of guidance from cadre, most of the local areas built their underground tunnels with one floor and few or no by-passages. The enemy will detect these underground tunnels easily and we will meet difficulties because of these deficiencies.

In order to permit safe and continuous fighting by our troops, they must be able to hide in another by-passage if one is discovered or escape to another floor if one is destroyed by the enemy. This explains the necessity for building an underground tunnel with several by-passages and floors. At the entrance to by-passages and separate floors, there must be covers and other materials for fire prevention.

c) Correct direction: There are two ways to maintain the right direction when we dig underground tunnels: with devices; with the manual procedure.

- **We introduce here the manual procedure:** After examining the terrain, studying the combat plan carefully and determining the dimensions, we begin to dig in many spots at the same time. It is difficult to make the two ends connect, of course, because our technical skill is poor and we lack facilities. To overcome this difficulty, we must dig many openings 20 to 30 metres apart and regulate the direction by producing sounds. NB: Nearby openings help us adjust the direction more easily, but they facilitate enemy detection, even if they are later filled up and camouflaged.

**2. Working methods:**

a) Design and marks: At first, the cadre must study the location carefully. Then, they plant banners, poles or reference sticks to mark the different areas as required by the combat plan: the entrance, the passages, the direction, the corners and so on. After that the digging may be started.

b) Disposition of manpower: From the moment they receive the mission, they must study the location, and examine the situation until they assign tasks and responsibilities to individuals.

The cadre must spend on this a considerable amount of time. We offer some suggestions as to an effective distribution of work, and hope that the local areas will gain more experience in the process of building their underground tunnels.

—two persons will dig and shovel earth from the tunnel

—one person will rake the earth out of the opening.

These three persons will rotate their work.

We do not mention the number of persons needed for removing the earth will be removed and thus depend on the specific local areas [sic]. 'Swing-excavators' [a bamboo crane-excavator] are desirable to remove the earth more quickly from the tunnels, because the roof of the tunnel must be 1.5 metres thick, so we must dig down into the ground to a depth of 2.5 to 3 metres.

In case the entrance of the underground tunnel cannot be located behind concealment, the diggers must fill superfluous openings according to the requirements of the combat plan. NB: There are two ways of placing the wooden supports or bamboo poles (10 centimetres in diameter) in the openings: place them horizontally; place them vertically. The wooden supports or bamboo poles are placed horizontally and close together in the opening. They are covered with bamboo wattles, then with a thick layer of clay, to prevent rainwater from entering. Over the layer of clay, another layer of well-pressed earth is added to make the openings level with the surface of the ground. Of course, the horizontal wooden struts or bamboo poles must have supports under them. The vertical struts or bamboo poles must also be placed close to each other. They are covered with well-pressed earth.

This method is only adopted when we must fill in the openings at the extreme ends [sic]. The layers of earth must be strongly pressed to prevent the enemy from discovering the many openings (in which case, he sets off mines and bangalores or pours smoke into the underground tunnels). The entrance to an underground tunnel is preferably located in bushy, concealed and unexpected places.

Not far from the entrance, there must be combat fortifications (or combat posts). Our soldiers will be able to fight from these posts before they enter the underground tunnel or after they leave it. The fortifications must not be too close to the entrance because they will betray its presence. Covert ways connecting them with the passages of the underground tunnel are also necessary.

c) The passages: The passages are dug in the following ways: with digging devices; with the hands. We introduce here the way to dig passages with the hands.

- Manual digging: The passages are usually dug by: two persons who rotate in digging and in shovelling the earth; two to three persons who remove the earth (depending on how far the earth must be removed). The total is four to five persons.
- Notice: The earth removed from the underground tunnel

should be made into basements for houses, furrows for potato growing or banks for communications and combat trenches. It may also be poured into streams but must never be left heaped in mounds. In short, the utmost care must be taken to conceal the underground tunnel from the enemy's discovery.

d) Equipment in the underground tunnel: As we know, the enemy is very dangerous. He drops hundreds of tons of bombs and fires thousands of shells on our villages to kill cattle and innocent victims. He also destroys the people's crops with chemicals. In sweep operations, the enemy soldiers try to destroy our underground tunnels by setting off mines and bangalores, or by pouring in chemicals, smoke or water. If we want to fight him both in the open and in underground tunnels, we need to equip them adequately. The underground tunnels are protected on the outside by combat posts, spike pits, mines and booby traps. They must also be well equipped inside for combat.

- Combat equipment: In emergencies, our troops enter underground tunnels. They must be able to continue fighting. To help them do so, we must build our underground tunnels with several by-passages, floors, openings and covers. At the corners and between the floors, there must be strong covers to protect us from mine and grenade fragments. We must also dig spike pits in underground tunnels which we cover normally for safety. We may also lay mines and grenade traps in advance but should not fix the wires. When the enemy enters the underground tunnel, we must be able to sneak into a by-passage or to another floor before the mines and grenades are set in the armed position. The covers will serve to protect our troops from smoke and chemicals. The following two ways are adopted for making covers:

With boards 1 centimetre thick and 2 to 3 centimetres wide, make two frames: one with horizontal boards and the other with vertical boards. Insert a nylon sheet between the two frames which later will be glued together. Cover it with sponge rubber and fill all openings with wax. NB: A single board should never be used for a frame, because it is not strong enough.

Another type of cover can be made in the form of a bottle cork. One man can sneak through the opening and shut the cover after him. NB: The cork must be covered with a plastic sheet.

- Equipment for activity: The underground tunnel must be well equipped inside, just as it is outside. There must be resting places, areas for wounded soldiers, food storage points, latrines and urinals, and ventilation shafts. (There must be several ventilation shafts turned towards the wind.) To prevent the underground tunnel from being flooded, a hollow must be dug every 20 to 30 metres. It should be 20 centimetres wide, 15 centimetres deep and serves to contain drain water.

Furthermore, we must prevent detection by the enemy's dogs and not allow snakes to enter the tunnels. For this purpose, we must scatter some garlic or powdered pepper at the entrance or near the ventilation shafts. NB: Avoid staying in groups. The dogs will detect our presence and the enemy will discover the underground tunnel more easily if we are in groups.

V. Camouflage

Camouflage is very important, because it reduces the number of the enemy's opportunities to discover our underground tunnel. We must think of camouflage continuously once the underground tunnel is built. It should be done so skilfully as to blend the entrance of the underground tunnel with the terrain and natural environment. Manioc or sweet potatoes may be grown on the entrance, as experience has proven. But the best way to maintain secrecy for the underground tunnel is, as ever, to indoctrinate the local people with a firm determination to turn deaf and dumb to the enemy's enquiries.

VI. Supervision and maintenance

Supervision and maintenance have recently been neglected in many local areas. Damaged areas were not discovered in time and repaired. We should therefore have specific plans for supervision and maintenance, and repair damage in case cave-ins or fissures occur (by making support frames).

Printed in Great Britain
by Amazon

43735014R00161